DIRT, RABBITS,

and

OTHER TWO-LEGGED VARMINTS

*short stories from a simpler
time and place*

DIRT, RABBITS,

and

OTHER TWO-LEGGED VARMINTS

*short stories from a simpler
time and place*

by Michael Hairgrove

Original drawings by Larry Neagle

ACKNOWLEDGMENTS

It would be impossible to list all the folks who contributed to this book. Many helpful hands and thoughtful friends helped me with this endeavor. Suffice it to say, I am most grateful for your help and support. The list, though, incomplete, follows:

Dr. Forrest Burt, a friend and colleague, encouraged everyone he met to strive for excellence. He was the type of person we'd all like to emulate.

Mr. Larry Neagle, a friend, mentor, teacher, and illustrator. His work taught me the 'nuts and bolts' of the creative process and helped make the book a reality.

Mrs. Sheila Fredrickson, friend and go-to person. She provided me with expertise and direction in the overall implementation of the book.

Finally, *Betty Hairgrove*, my companion and the love of my life. She always encouraged and supported me in my various projects. Her spirit lives on as my inspiration.

CONTENTS

MISS LILLIAN'S REVENGE

"Tuffy" Smith was christened 'Caesar Augustus' by his mother. Born prematurely, Lula Mae Smith hoped he'd grow into his name. Weighing less than four pounds at birth, Tuffy spent his life trying to catch up with his name. When he was in high school, his 5'4" frame, black hair and eyes made him attractive to all the girls, but fame and fortune eluded him.

In fact, he got his nickname from attempting to take someone's girl friend away from her beau. Whenever a fight occurred, he lost every time, only winning the sympathy of the girls who thought of him as a romantic lover, not a fighter.

In his early thirties, Tuffy did not settle for marriage. He still wanted to drink, dance and carouse with as many women as he could. He managed to keep his boyish good looks, and learned to avoid as many fights with husbands as possible.

During this time in his life, Tuffy met a new nurse who had returned to the community of Red Mud. Her father, recognizing that his daughter might not marry, sent her to nursing school in Lubbock. After three years, she graduated and returned home, living on the home place with her parents.

Attempting to modernize his practice, the country doctor, Doc. Hall built a two-story, fifteen-bed hospital. In the center of the hospital, a wide staircase led down to the emergency, or operating room, accessible from both floors. The cost of a room was fifteen dollars in 1920; Dr. Hall hadn't changed his prices in thirty years, believing that he was performing a public service to the citizens of Red Mud.

As soon as Dr. Hall heard that Lillian was available, he hired her as his primary nurse. Upon seeing Lillian at the Red Front Drug Store talking with her friends, Tuffy decided to make another conquest. He walked over to the counter at the soda fountain and said, "Hello, beautiful."

Not knowing that he was talking to her, Lillian ignored him.

She's playing hard to get. "I don't believe we've met. I'm Tuffy Smith. There's a dance at Roaring Springs Saturday night and I'd like to take you."

He is good looking in those tight jeans. I bet he can really dance. It might be fun to go with him, though Daddy has told me about his reputation.

Not wanting her family to know about Tuffy, she said, "All right. Where shall we meet? I live nine miles out of town. Do you want me to meet you someplace here in town?"

"That would be nice. Let's meet here at the drug store. See you around seven. That will give us plenty of time to get to the dance. See you then."

As Tuffy turned to leave, Barbara asked Lill, "What are you doing? He's the biggest Romeo in these parts. I can think of at least four girls who had to drop out of high school and go to Lubbock to have their babies. He hasn't helped a single one of them."

"Well, this is different. I'm going to have a good time. I know better than to expect much from Tuffy."

Tuffy and Lillian had many dates. In January, they couple went to the Fort Worth Fat Stock Show; in the spring, they attended the rodeos in Stamford and other neighboring communities. They were inseparable at watermelon parties, dances and taffy pulls. In no time at all, Lillian fell under Tuffy's spell. When Miss Lill had to work the night shift, she suspected that Tuffy took someone else to wine and dine. Afraid of finding out about Tuffy's other dates, Lill never confronted him.

Her parents worried, though, tried to talk to her, and prayed a lot. The dates and conquests became more important to Tuffy than having a steady girl, so Miss Lill eventually told him good-bye. Sorry that her parents were correct, she swore off all men, choosing to make her nursing career the vital part of her life.

Time had not been kind to Tuffy. All the drinking, lack of sleep, and dissipation caused him to look older than he was. When he was in his forties, he went to a dance, got drunk, and proposed to a rancher's daughter. Awakening the next morning to find he was married, Tuffy's life changed.

Never a beauty, Belle, his wife, had lost the good-looks that men notice years ago. Having a slight paunch, blonde hair and green eyes, she dressed in clothes that did not display her best features. Reared on a ranch, she could ride, rope and brand cattle. She was a head taller than Tuffy and out-weighed him by fifty pounds.

"Dear," she said, "I want you to find a good job and make some money. Now that I am married, I want to have a large family, and I want to start right now. Do you hear me?"

Tuffy heard, but his heart was not in getting a job. His friends, family, and occasionally, the girls he dated gave him money. "Yes, honey."

He couldn't figure out why his charm no longer worked on the women.

Enjoying a good time, Belle could match Tuffy drink-for-drink. As soon as she was pregnant, she insisted that both of them quit alcohol and save their money for a baby bed.

"Tuffy, get out of bed and get your ass in gear. There are plenty of jobs you could do, providing you weren't so lazy. I'm ashamed that Mama and Daddy are still having to help us ten years after we married. Now, I want you to get out there and start to make a living. Do you hear me?"

"Yes, Dear."

"And, another thing. If I hear of you flirting with another woman, I'll break your neck. Do you hear me?"

Tuffy heard, but he didn't like the news. "Yes, Sugar."

"And another thing: I had better not hear of you spending your money on beer. That money you have is for groceries and baby food."

"Yes, Dear."

Where did all the romance and good times go? I feel like a hound dog beaten down and cowed. Four kids later, nearly fifty, in-laws on my case, and there's no fun in living. There's got to be more to life than this. I miss the good old times.

Tuffy had a three-week job helping repair a fence on a neighboring ranch. He didn't mind working hard; he minded having to give his money to Belle. Deciding to recapture the good old days when he finished the job, Tuffy thanked Mr. Green for the pay check. As soon as he got

into his pickup, Tuffy headed for the liquor store. He passed Belle heading for Mr. Green's spread in her old '37 Chevy.

She wants my check and I beat her to it this time.

When Belle found out that Tuffy had the money, she knew where he was headed. With four squalling kids in the back seat, she turned the car around and headed for the store.

"Tuffy, you take that beer right back in there and get your money back."

"I can't do that, I've already opened two cans."

"Then you head for the house. This discussion is not over."

Like a gambler caught cheating at cards, Tuffy got in the pickup and started for home. Belle followed closely behind. Before reaching the house, Tuffy managed to put away two more beers. Not quite in a mellow mood, he dreaded the lecture that was to come. He certainly hadn't captured the good old days. Placing the remainder of the case on the table, he sat down to await the sermon.

"How could you take the baby's food from her? What did you think we were going to do for rent money? How could you be so irresponsible?"

Sorrowfully looking up at her, Tuffy said, "I miss having fun. You won't let me do anything that I used to do. All you ever do is nag, nag, nag."

"Well, I wouldn't have to if you had a backbone and took some responsibility for your family."

"You take enough responsibility for both of us. At least, leave me alone and let me drink in peace."

Seeing red, Belle picked up one of the empty bottles, "I'll leave you in peace, you low-down skunk."

With that comment, she aimed the bottle at Tuffy. He raised his arm to protect himself, saw the bottle approaching and ducked the first swing. Missing the initial swipe of the bottle, Tuffy felt the full impact of the second one. The blow struck him across the mouth, breaking a tooth and splitting his lip. Blood was gushing from the wound.

"Why, you ungrateful bitch." Tuffy slapped Belle with his free arm.

The fight was basically over; the pain in Tuffy's face and the excess bleeding made Tuffy withdraw.

When Cleo Lassiter, the local constable, arrived, he saw Belle's eye turning blue and Tuffy's lip bleeding. "I've got a call about a domestic disturbance."

Looking around, he said, "Tuffy, what on earth happened to you?"

Belle said, "Cleo, I want that no-good skunk arrested for threatening me and the kids."

"All right. Maybe a night in the jail will calm both of you down. But first, we've got to stop that bleeding."

Picking up his radio to inform the dispatcher, Cleo said, "Mable, I'm bringing Tuffy in, but we need to stop by the hospital for some patching up. Is Doc. Hall still there?"

"No, I bet he's gone home, but Miss Lillian can take care of you."

At those words, Tuffy's eyes widened. "Cleo, please don't let Miss Lill get hold of me."

"Why," asked Cleo. "She's a good nurse and will fix you up in no time."

After driving up to the hospital, Cleo led Tuffy to the emergency room. The hospital was quiet. With the evening meal over, the patients settled in for the night.

"Well, hello, Constable. What have we here?"

"Evening, Miss Lill. Tuffy here got in a fight with his wife and needs some one to work on him."

"Was he drinking?" asked Miss Lill, talking directly to Cleo.

"Yes, Ma'm."

"Then he doesn't need any pain medicine. Sit him down over there and I'll get the needle and thread."

"Miss Lill, please don't hurt me. Miss Lill, please don't hurt me. I'm sorry. I didn't mean to get into a fight. Please be gentle."

Choosing the largest needle for the job, Miss Lill chose not to use any pain-killer on his lip. She attacked the job as a contest between good and evil.

After a few seconds, a loud, low scream permeated the hospital.

"Damn you, bitch. I asked you to be good to me. Please don't hurt me again. Please, Lill, please."

After a pause, another low, deep scream could be heard in the hospital.

"You sorry bitch. I begged you not to hurt me. Now, please, please don't hurt me, Miss Lill. Remember the good old times."

Looking at Tuffy, she said, "I am remembering the old times."

"Cleo," said Miss Lillian, "hold him steady, he keeps trying to move away from the needle."

"Yes, Ma'm."

Once again, pleadings arose while Nurse Lillian took aim.

"You sorry piece of humanity. I begged you not to hurt me, and you did it again. I hope you rot in hell for the way you treat me. Come on, Constable, get me away from the clutches of that butcher."

"Thank you, Miss Lill. Send the bill to the court house."

Stepping into the emergency room from behind the door, Belle spotted Miss Lill. She had followed Cleo's car to the hospital.

"Are you all right, Belle?" asked Miss Lill.

"Yes, I have a bloody nose and a black eye, but I'll be fine. Thanks for the job you just finished on Tuffy."

"Hon, I did it for women everywhere. You're welcome," said Nurse Lillian.

PIE IN THE SKY

Spitting, and whittling, Joe Bob Richards and Billy Edwards, two dry land farmers in Comanche County, were sitting under the oak trees surrounding the courthouse. August was always hot, offering little relief from the dry weather. Joe Bob stopped whittling a moment to strop his pocket knife.

"What did that fellow from Dyess Air Force Base want with Leon?" he asked.

Billy spit some tobacco juice at a nearby grasshopper. "Well, the story I heard was that every time the planes flew over Leon's farm, especially over his dirt tank, the gauges on the planes started spinning. It seems like the mud in the stock tank is radioactive. In fact, I hear that when his cows drank from the tank, they gave radioactive milk."

"So, what?" asked Joe Bob.

"Well, the colonel got permission to take samples back to the air base. The tests showed that there is uranium in the soil. That means Old Leon will be rich, if the find is big."

"What do they want with uranium?" asked Joe Bob.

"The government uses it to make nuclear bombs."

Joe Bob shook his head. "Fat lot of good that will do us. With the crops burning up, I guess we can just sit back and watch Old Leon get rich off the dirt tank." Joe Bob snapped a chunk out of his whittling stick. He tried to shape his stick so that it looked like something, unlike some men who just wanted to reduce a stick to shavings. So far, he'd been unsuccessful.

After examining his last cut, he muttered, "Do you suppose Leon would sell some of his land, or share some of his dirt with us?"

Billy wiped his forehead with a dirty handkerchief. "It wouldn't hurt to ask. In fact, I see his old Ford pickup at the grocery store now. I guess he and Bertha Jean are buying a bill of groceries. Let's mosey over and talk to him."

Both men walked stiff-legged until the circulation started flowing in their legs. Walking slowly, they reached the pickup. Joe Bob tipped his hat. " Howdy, Ms. Hill," said Joe Bob, Then turning to face Leon, Joe Bob continued, "Leon, I heard about your good luck. Billy and I wondered if we could be of assistance in this deal you got with the gov'ment."

Leon set a box of canned goods on the truck bed. "Well, I don't know what you've heard, but there is no deal. I got a letter from the Department of Defense yesterday telling me the uranium was no good. The grade is so poor that the government isn't interested. If things had been different, the government would buy all I could supply. Now, it looks like another dry hole."

Joe Bob felt some of the wind go out of his sails. "I'm sorry to hear that, Leon. Maybe we could try something else. It may not be good for bomb-making, but do your cows really give radioactive milk?"

"Now, that is just plain foolishness."

"What if we told people that they did?" asked Billy.

"Well, ten old milk cows couldn't give enough milk to make much money. Besides, who would want to drink it?"

Joe Bob chewed on the end of his whittling stick, thinking, "What if we got people to sit in the dirt—for medicinal reasons only, mind you?"

"What's medicinal about sitting in dirt?" Bertha Jean snapped.

"And, who in their right mind would want to?" added Leon.

"Well, remember that Indian fellow in Oklahoma that poured liquor in a bottle and sold a ton of it for home remedies? He tripled the price he got for moonshine by selling it as medicine. A lot of church women swore by its healing effects."

Bertha Jane piped up, "Listen, I've heard of big city women who put mud on their faces to make themselves beautiful. But what normal person would wallow in the mud, just like an old hog?"

With an air of propriety, Billy said, "I don't think I would want *my* wife to get down and dirty in a pile of dirt. It isn't dignified for womenfolk."

"Then we're going to have to emphasize the medical part of it. We'll make it like a sanitarium," said Joe Bob, "and, what if it really did them some good? Besides, we could use the dirt over and over. It wouldn't be like selling the milk one time."

"Well," said Bertha Jean, " the women won't want to take their clothes off. It's not decent. I can imagine all the sermons preached about this pile of iniquity," said Bertha.

"If the customers were wrapped in sheets, fully dressed, that should satisfy everyone," said Leon, warming to the idea. "Now, the question is, where do we want to build the clinic?"

"Leon," piped Bertha, "is this just another hairbrained notion you've let yourself get talked into? Why on earth don't you stop and think about it?"

"As I said earlier, " said Joe Bob, "Billy and I could help you with this deal for shares in it. The cost of starting up the business would be minimal, since you've already got the dirt. It could really be a money-maker for all of us."

"Yes," said Bertha Jane, "or just another piece of foolishness."

The following morning, over a cup of steaming coffee, Leon addressed his partners. "I think it's a good idea. If we lose money, it won't be much, and, it just might work. The first thing we need, though, is a building for a clinic."

Joe Bob said, "I've got an old hen house we could move over here. It would take some renovating, but we could build individual stalls for the patients."

"Also, we could give the customer what he wants: if he has a sore toe, he could stick his foot in the dirt; if he has an arthritic knee, he could cover his knee," said Billy.

Taking notes on a yellowed Big Chief tablet, Leon said, "Now we've got it, but we've got to get some testimonials. Who do we know that is so crippled up that any improvement in his health would be a miracle?" asked Leon.

Joe Bob guffawed, "That'd be Old Man Jones. He uses a cane and a crutch. He is so crippled up from arthritis he should be glad for any relief. Besides, I know for a personal fact that he once bought a gallon jug of medicine from the man in Oklahoma and swore it helped him."

After moving the old chicken house, and by working steadily for three weeks, the men were open for business.

They replaced the chicken wire with stalls made of two-by-fours. A second, white coat of paint gave it a 'hospital' look. The sign above the door, painted by a professional, proclaimed to the world: "The Uranium Sitting House, Ltd." The "Ltd." was added by Joe Bob who had read it somewhere.

An ad in the town's paper heralded the opening. As expected, the town gossips, the nosey neighbors, and word-of-mouth caused a commotion. Among the first patients was Mr. Jones, who asked for the full treatment of one hour of dirt sitting for one dollar.

After one treatment, Mr. Jones said, "I'll tell you fellows, if I'd had a place like this twenty years ago, I wouldn't have gotten so crippled up. I feel like a new man. I may use all my pension money on your business."

The novelty of dirt sitting caused the business to grow beyond their expectations. Almost overnight, the parking lot was full. Cars parked in the pasture, around the house, anywhere the customer could find space. For hours and hours, people lined up and paid their hard-earned money for the opportunity of feeling young again.

⸺ ◅◆◆◅ ⸺

After spending the better part of a month working twelve-hour days, the boys were thinking of expanding. Then one day, Leon came running up to greet them. Holding a letter, he said, "Fellows, I got an invite to appear on the television. When Earl Duncan came home last weekend, he heard about our sitting house. When he got back to Fort Worth, he told his boss.

The station wants me to tell about our operation. On T.V. Think of the publicity. Why, nothing like this has ever happened in the United States in 1950. We are riding the crest of a mighty wave of health cures."

"Yes," said Joe Bob, "and making a killing at it, too."

Smiling, Leon said, "Yeah. Ain't it nice?"

⸺ ◅◆◆◅ ⸺

Bertha Jean led Leon into the T.V. station. They'd arrived on time, no thanks to Leon.

He'd wasted the better part of a half hour trying to leave her behind. She'd straightened him out on that.

Sitting beside Leon in the broadcast studio, she straightened out a wrinkle in her best, hand-sewn, Gladiola, flour-sack dress.

After the pork futures were read, the farm director said, "Folks, I'm honored today to have a special guest, Mr. Leon Hill. He drove all the way from Comanche this morning to be with us." Looking at Leon, he extended his hand.

Leon stared at the camera, and didn't move. Bertha Jean could see the panic written on his face. As the camera moved toward him for a close up, she nudged him sharply with her elbow. Leon opened his mouth, but his voice failed him. Bertha Jean had seen that same expression on his face at their wedding. A deer in a pickup's headlights displayed less terror.

The farm director broke for a quick commercial. Bertha Jean was afraid, but she wasn't about to let Leon ruin her chance of being on television. She elbowed Leon again and told the farm director, "When the commercial ends, talk to me."

Fifteen seconds later, he said, "Mrs. Hill, could you tell us about your new business?"

Steeling up her courage, Bertha replied, "We have a uranium sitting house on the farm.

Folks come from all over the county to sit in our dirt. The uranium is guaranteed to cure lumbago, tuberculosis, emphysema, and arthritis."

"Where did you find the dirt?"

"We got it from our stock tank in the pasture."

"How did you know it had uranium in the dirt?"

"A man from the government came and tested it. The uranium doesn't have enough strength to make bombs or harm people, just enough to make them well."

"What happens when your livestock drink out of that tank?

"There's been reports of the milk being radioactive, but I don't believe a word of it; the cows don't glow at night and neither do Leon or myself."

"How does the dirt work?"

"People coming in for a treatment can either sit down or lie down, and are then covered up in clean sheets. Our attendants then cover the patients with dirt. The treatment generally takes an hour."

"Do you know of anyone who has had a miracle cure?"

Warming up to the topic, Bertha nodded, "Why, yes. Luther Joe Slaton got cured of warts. That boy was an awful mess before his treatments. He had warts all over his face. Now, it is as clear as a baby's behind."

"Could you give any other accounts of miracles at your business?"

"Yes, sir. Old man C.C. Jones, a good Christian man who doesn't lie, was crippled up with arthritis so bad he could barely get into the dirt for his first treatment. That gimpy leg he has was caused when a mule kicked him. Today, he walks without a cane or a crutch."

"Well. There you have it, folks. Why not take a little ride and be refreshed? What a wonderful new idea for

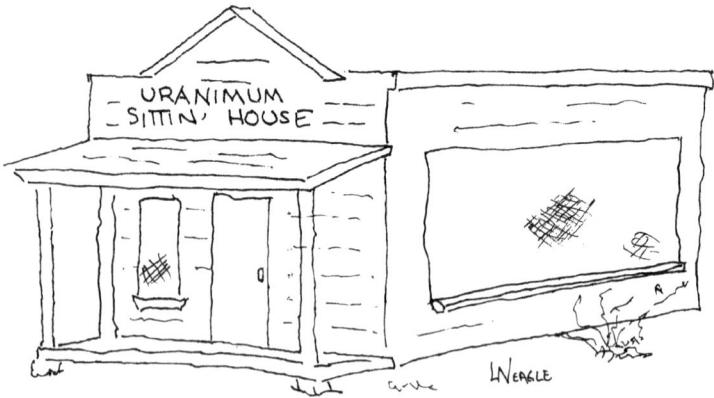

making a living on the farm. I sure am glad you folks could visit with us."

———— ⊗⊗⊗ ————

According to the local press, Bertha was a celebrity. *The local Uranium Sitting House establishment now has a spokesman on television. Our own Bertha Hill, daughter of Homer and Lula Jay, wife of Leon Hill appeared on the farm show in Fort Worth last Tuesday morning. Reports are that she was very eloquent and a credit to our community."*

———— ⊗⊗⊗ ————

As soon as the couple drove up to their house from the interview, Joe Bob handed Leon a letter. Other speculators wanted to buy dirt and start their own sitting houses, from as far away as Crosbyton and Sweetwater. The men from

Weatherford decided to issue stock in their project and hoped to become wealthy. "What should we do, Leon? Would you be willing to sell some dirt and earn extra money?"

"Sure," said Leon, " provided we still have enough for ourselves."

"While you were out, I took a call from Robert Taylor, the movie star. He wanted an appointment on Thursday. He's going to fly into Abilene and rent a car. I told him we'd have a stall for him whenever he arrived."

Bertha said, "We need to treat him right. If the movie stars start coming for treatments, we should go up on our prices, say fifty cents an hour more."

Robert Taylor, Barbara Stanwick, Mickey Rooney, Robert Cummings, Tom Mix and others came. The stars came for different reasons: the women wanted to remain young and beautiful. Tom said he came to get the kinks out of his hide from making all those action films. Along with their autographs, each movie star's picture was added to the "Wall of Stars." The pictures drew as many people as the treatments.

Ray Don Howell, an investigative reporter on the Abilene News, heard about the uranium sitting house in Comanche. He smelled news. And it wasn't good news. Getting permission from the editor, Ray Don drove around Texas for a couple of weeks.

Upon returning to his desk, Ray Don was asked about his findings. "What have you learned?" asked the editor.

"There's low grade uranium all over Texas, including the stones used to build the state capitol. Leaning against the stones at the capitol building in Austin offers a greater chance of helping people than the dirt they sit in in Comanche."

"You mean to tell me the sitting house story ranks up there with the Okie and his potion, or some snake oil salesman?'

"Afraid so."

"What about the believers who swore the sitting house helped them?"

"I sure hope they didn't throw their crutches and canes away."

───────── ⌾⌾⌾ ─────────

Despite widespread publicity to the contrary, the Sitting House of Comanche survived six more months before closing.

───────── ⌾⌾⌾ ─────────

GOODBYE TO BUTTERCUP

Clomping through the back door, Wilburn slowly removed his dirty, old straw hat, hanging it on a nail. He stepped into the kitchen, as he did everyday for the past fifty years. Steaming on the stove, the smells of fried steak, potatoes and gravy permeated the kitchen. The fresh corn on the cob and the juicy tomatoes picked fresh this morning rounded out the noon meal. Judith began piling his plate when she heard the back screen close.

"Did the mail come yet?"

"Yes, I picked it up on my way from the garden."

"Was there any news, or was it just duns and circulars?"

"There's a letter from Cindy."

"Trouble at school, or with her boyfriend?"

"Not that I can tell. You read it."

Wilburn put his fork back on the table and slowly read the letter. Finishing, he grinned at Judith. "She wants to sell Buttercup again. I declare, that girl is always looking for ways to spend money."

"Will, it's time you got shed of that goat and put a stop to this nonsense. I can't remember the number of times I've given you my egg money, so Cindy could buy some foolishness."

"It sounds like school is going well. She likes her teachers, but she needs a new dress for some party."

"So, Buttercup's head is on the block again, huh?"

"Well, you are the bookkeeper, but surely we have enough to help that girl out. Can we send her what she wants, without selling the old goat?" asked Wilburn.

"Now, Will, you aren't getting my egg money again. The trouble I go to, you would spend every dime I have on Cindy, just because she is our granddaughter. You need to tell her, we can barely pay the taxes on this poor dry-land farm, much less have money for Cindy."

"Now, Ma," Wilburn said gently, picking his fork up to begin again. "You know Cindy is sensible and only spends for what she needs. After all, Buttercup really belongs to her. She was only a little tyke when we gave her the goat and she can sell it at anytime. That was the agreement, remember?"

"I remember when she got the goat. You both were silly over that runt the nanny goat didn't want. I also remember all the times she wrote and asked you to sell Buttercup, only to have you send money."

Will mulled over Judith's comments. Cindy's mom, Barbara, their only daughter, left the farm years ago and married a no-good salesman who was never home. She divorced when Cindy was only four. Spending summers on the farm, Cindy and Will became buddies, sharing their joy in the birth of the chicks, ducks, and kids. Cindy's job was to tend to the animals. When she forgot or daydreamed, Will took care of it. Judith knew of the arrangement between the two, feeling that Will spoiled her too much.

"You should never have given her the goat. That's where the problem all started. Whenever Barbara couldn't afford to buy school clothes, Cindy would ask Grandpa and you'd pretend to sell that old goat."

"Well, the plan worked. Cindy got money for school, including clothes, cosmetics, and shoes. Besides, I enjoyed seeing her enjoy herself."

LNEAGLE

"It worked as long as the hens laid, but what are we going to do now that you're sick? If you had gone to the doctor sooner, things would be different."

"Now, Ma, we've survived too many sandstorms and droughts to think much could go wrong with me, except maybe getting old."

Combined with a distrust of doctors and work to be done, Will waited until his condition was serious. Judith, his wife of forty-six years, could do little to persuade him, once his mind was closed. Wilburn would see the doctor when the crop was gathered.

The other major problem was Buttercup. Will named all the livestock and became attached to them. If an animal remained six months, it received a name: milk cows, goats, geese, and chickens—none was exempt.

Buttercup was different. Being the only animal to reciprocate Will's feelings, she grew close. After giving the goat to Cindy, Will made up his mind to ignore Buttercup, but Buttercup's first love was Will. Trotting up whenever Wilburn appeared, Buttercup followed him as he did the chores. They were a curious pair; she, following him around like a puppy, and he, patting and talking to her as if she understood every word he said.

Will swore that Buttercup knew him better than Ma. She, at least, did not object to his dipping snuff and spitting.

Judith was the other problem. Dedicating her life to cleaning house, she endured sandstorms, tornadoes, and Wilburn's tobacco habit. Her passport to heaven consisted of cleaning her house, and she intended to keep her passport current. Judith's concession to Will's habit was to keep an empty can by his chair, when he needed to spit.

In time, the bond between Buttercup and Wilburn grew, so whenever Cindy wrote and asked to sell her goat, Will managed to find the money and send it to her, thus sparing them both the heart-wrenching separation.

Before the crop was gathered, Judith had to drive Will to the hospital. Tests were made; the condition was terminal. After the exploratory surgery, Will was sewn up and sent home. Judith met with the doctor on the day Will was released.

"There's not much else we can do. Keep him quiet and help him enjoy his last days."

"Does he know how bad it is?"

"He suspects as much, but he is very weak and attributes his feeling bad to the surgery."

While in the hospital, Will missed his buddy, and Buttercup was lonely for her best friend. Both of them brightened up when Buttercup spied his old Ford pickup approaching the gate to their home. Waiting patiently for Will at the gate was Buttercup.

"Can we stop a minute to speak to Buttercup?"

"No, and don't act silly. You're in no shape to walk over and waste time with that smelly, old goat."

"Female goats don't smell; it's the males that have an odor. Besides, can't you see how happy she is to see me? If you won't stop at the gate, maybe she can meet me at the front porch by the fence."

"I don't want her around the house. It is just as well she stay out in the pasture. Besides, we've got to think about what's best for you." Judith's love for Will was abiding; her tolerance for Buttercup was wearing thin.

"I know what's best for me." Will muttered under his breath. "Judith, I need to see Joe Bob so we can talk about getting the crop gathered. Will you have him come by?"

Joe Bob, his neighbor for over forty years, came by the following morning.

"Will you help me get Judith out of the house?"

"Will, I'd be happy to, but I sure don't want her to turn on me. What have you got in mind?"

"Go to the barn and find a worn-out part on that old F-16 Farmall tractor. That's the easy part. Then tell her you need her to go to town to replace the part that is broken. Tell her you'd go, but you need to finish the chores and you can't afford to lose the daylight."

The next afternoon, Joe Bob came into the bedroom. "Will, your plan worked. Judith is on her way to the implement shop. Now, what do you want from me?"

"I want to see Buttercup and tell her to be a good girl."

Dreading Judith's wrath, Joe Bob fetched Buttercup, who was waiting near the front porch. Opening the gate nearest the house, Buttercup followed him expectantly. When Joe Bob opened the screen door, Buttercup ran into the kitchen. Through the bedroom door, Buttercup spied

Will. She bounded into the room, jumped on the bed, gently nudging Will.

"Well, old girl, you are looking good. How have you been?" Not waiting for a reply, Will scratched behind her ears and the two carried on an animated conversation: Buttercup's eyes were dancing and Will was explaining his situation to her. The two communicants were temporarily ecstatic, not expecting Judith to return so quickly.

"I'll not have that darned old goat in my house. Do you hear me? If it happens one more time, we'll have bar-be-cued goat, or her new home will be at Joe Bob's."

Will smiled, contentedly, "Yes, dear."

Buttercup returned to the barn, one happy goat. She was permanently furloughed to Joe Bob's farm, shortly after Will's funeral.

After catching Will in bed with Buttercup, Judith, using her egg money, bought herself a new, store-bought dress, as agreed to by both parties, the result of Wilburn's dalliance.

ANGELITA'S CHOICE

Sitting on the edge of her narrow bed, one thin leg crossed under the other, Angelita stared absently through the worn and soiled sheets wrinkling about her body.

The drab room enveloped her in shades of dingy light and fading dark—all approaching a brown sameness. Threadbare, never-laundered curtains held years of street dust. A few checkered splotches of linoleum clung to the dry, plank floor. A straight chair stood beside the door to the hallway, and atop a scratched table squatted a kerosene lamp with a battered shade.

A crucifix hung high above the headboard of Angelita's bed. Beneath it, a veladora, with its wax-encrusted apron showed heavy use; its solitary candle awaited the next strike of a match, the next prayer. Only these two objects broke the silence of the walls. Only these, and Angelita, drew the eyes.

Cocooned in a rolled-up rag, pushed to the back of the table's only drawer, a corn-husk doll slept in cloistered darkness.

— Angelita's Choice —

The frail, fifteen-year-old watched from the bed as dusk enlarges the dark spaces in the sky. The glitzy, Christmas lights came on outside, disguising the rough realities of the building. The year-round decorations, designed to look festive, put the customer in a buying mood.

From time to time, she laboriously studied the short letter that arrived that day, attempting to recall the words that Sra. Garcia read to her. The letter told her that Lupe, her younger sister was coming, and Angelita's job was to be at the station tomorrow.

My dear little Angel:
Father Tomas is writing this note for me. Times are very
hard. We need rain for the animals. Without the animals,
we have no money. I am sending Guadalupe on the train
to work with you. Meet the train on Wednesday.
Love, Papa

Two years ago, Angelita had come to the border town of Nuevo Laredo from her home in the Chihuahuan desert. Born premature, she had started life in an uneven fight and continued to struggle. Too frail to watch the goats or even do housework, Angelita depended upon her parents, Emanuel and Josefina, to make choices for her. The last of their choices sent her to the city to earn money in a bordello.

"Angelita?"

"Yes, Papa?"

"Mi Cielo, you know that there is little food."

"Yes, Papa," she said.

"Mama and I have decided that you are to go to Nuevo Laredo to work."

"What, Papa?"

"It is time for you to leave home to help the family."

"But, Papa, I have never been away from my family or my home. What am I to do? How will I know what to do? I am afraid."

"Do you remember Maria Garcia? Her family lived down the creek from our house? Well, in 1938, she moved to Nuevo Laredo to find work. Now, she hires young girls like you to help her. Your mama will go with you on the train. She will stay with you until you get settled."

"Can't I stay here? I promise not to eat much." Angelita replied.

"No, the matter is settled. I will miss my little angel." Papa struggled to finish what he is saying: "But I know you will be all right."

Angelita, always an obedient child, trusted. I should do as I am told. I am glad Mama is going with me. There is so much to learn and see.

Angelita told her pet rooster Rafael goodbye, and then embraced her little brothers and sisters.

The next day, holding Angeita's arm and picking up the cardboard suitcase, Josefina started down the dirt trail to the train station, her flowered canvas purse dangling on her arm.

"I expect my little girl to always be…a good girl." Emanuel called out with tears in his eyes. "Cuidate, nina. Guardate to alma."

"Yes, Papa." answered his angel, fiercely hugging her corn-husk doll and clinging to Josefina.

Take care of myself. Guard my soul.

A half-hour walk in the hot sand brought mother and child to the train stop.

The locomotive stopped at intervals in the desert. At their stop, a tin roof provided shelter from the hot sun. The steam whistle belched, scaring Angelita, as the train begrudgingly slowed to a stop.

Noticing the questioning eyes of the two passengers, the conductor said, "The third class section is in the next car. You may pay me as soon as we get moving again. May I help you, little girl? The steps are very high."

"Thank you," Angelita said, "Hurry, Mama, I want you to go ahead."

The train jerked and quarreled as it left the station, reversing its strange arrival behavior. Once under way, Josefina purchased two tickets: one round-trip and a one-way.

"Mija, you sit next to the window."

"Mama, there is so much to see. How far the sun goes to hide behind the mountains. How beautiful. Like home."

Opening her purse, taking out some beans rolled inside tortillas, Josephina said "I don't want you to get sick by eating too much; we have twenty-four hours on the train."

"But, Mama," Angelita gently protested, "How can you talk of eating and sleeping when there is so much to see? I want to remember what it all looks like."

The train made numerous stops between Chihuahua and Nuevo Laredo. Angelita spent these intervals absorbed in watching men and women leaving or boarding.

Women emerged or approached wearing full, flowered skirts in bright blues and reds, intricately embroidered blouses, silver-trimmed leather belts. Their hair was knotted in long braids, twisting around their heads, or discreetly covered by long flowing scarves. Other women wore dark dresses and had wrapped themselves in their rebozos. Still others wore tailored suits.

How will I dress in the city?

Many men wore sombreros, but others had dirty cloth hats, while some bared their bald heads, unruly to the sun and wind. Campesinos, in their white shirts and pants, had knotted colored scarves. From other cars, men got on and off the train in suits, and some sported bright yellow or green shirts. Most had long and unruly moustaches.

Different from Papa's.

When the train stopped, vendors would board with their wares of candy, goat cheese, or trinkets, and then hurriedly depart. The view grew monotonous to her, the scenery a repetitious blend of sagebrush, sand, and low hills. Angelita tried to count the concrete electric posts parading past the windows. At last, she fell asleep, exhausted, unable to remember all that she had seen.

Arriving at Nuevo Laredo mid-morning, Josefina asked directions to the Zona de Tolerancia, a twenty-acre, walled district adjoining the town. Everyone knew its location. Josefina asked the policeman at the gate for the address of la duena, Sra. Garcia. After walking down the narrow street, she and Angelita arrived.

Recognizing an old friend, Josefina Lopez said, "Maria, this is my daughter, Angelita." Turning to Angelita, she said, "Angelita, this is Sra. Garcia."

"You must be weary from your trip. Come in and have coffee with me. Did you have any difficulty finding me?"

"No, we simply followed the directions of the ticket master at the station."

After serving the coffee, Sra. Garcia scrutinized Angelita.

"You are truly a little angel. Many girls arrive badly treated; you do not bear the scars of life yet. You are still beautiful. You will have your own room, taking your meals with me, until you learn to cook. If you have problems with the hombres, you come to me. Josefina, I will watch over her. You need not worry. Each week she will send money home."

Josefina accepted the arrangements. After hurriedly looking at Angelita's room, emptying and keeping the cardboard suitcase, she turned to leave. Josefina held her daughter for a moment, averting her eyes from Angelita's gaze and started for home.

That was two years ago. Now Lupe was coming on the train.

On the day of her arrival, Angelita decided to walk bare-footed to the depot. She should save her shoes for

Sunday. The warm sand felt good between her toes. She didn't have to be in a hurry. A breeze lightly caressed her face.

Like Sunday walks at home.

"Lupe, over here. My, you look so grown up since I last saw you. How is everyone? How is Rafael?"

"Angelita, I am so glad to see you." Setting down the cardboard suitcase, she continued, "Your old rooster Rafael misses you. Things are very bad. Papa has sold half of his goats and all the sheep. The men in the plaza were saying that was the worst year they can remember. We would have eaten your rooster, but Mama thinks he is too old and tough." Lupe laughed, "So we kept him. We need rain. Roberto and Martin lost their jobs on the big ranch. Papa watches the clouds and prays to la Virgencita. Mama is always the same; she believes the family will make it somehow."

Angelita saw her life through the eyes of her younger sister. The novelty of her city life had changed to despair as thick as a muddy road. The little girl who left home two years ago had become an adult, more than an adult, older. She did not want this life for Lupe.

"Are you hungry, or tired?"

"I am too excited to eat. Show me where I will live."

The introductions were made, Sra. Garcia told the girls they would have adjoining rooms and could cook their meals together. Each resident was provided an open, charcoal stove.

"Pretty girls soon marry a rich hombre and leave this place. I am surprised Angelita has stayed as long."

— Angelita's Choice —

"Thank you," Angelita smiled quietly.

Alone, with Angelita at the door between their rooms, Lupe asked, "Oh, Angelita, what must I do here?"

"The job is easy. Always make the hombre feel like you are having a good time. Most are not interested in talking. They want their money's worth. Remember to thank the hombre. He may return. Sra. Garcia will tell everyone you are a virgin. Men pay more for virgins. I pretended to be one for six months until someone complained."

Guadalupe looked around both of the drab rooms.

"We sleep in the daytime, and on Sunday, we can have picnics or go to the plaza. We don't get busy until the lights come on at dark. You must never let an hombre hurt you; tell Mama Garcia immediately."

Reflecting about what Mama Garcia said, Lupe asked, "Angelita, if I marry before you and leave, what will you do?"

"I intend to work hard, save my money, and leave on my own."

Lupe became accustomed to the routine and, by living frugally, accumulated some savings, sending money home. Being prettier than Angelita, Lupe was requested more often. The hombres with less money usually went with Angelita.

"Angelita, look at this sore on my neck. What is it?"

"Lupe, it is nothing. It will soon go away. Some young girls have pimples on their skin as they grow up. If it doesn't get better, we will go see Sra. Esperanza, the curandera. She worked here, but now she is old: she sells trinkets and herbs that help people. She has the reputation of knowing cures. She is a good healer."

Appearing as bruises, the lesions, dark-colored splotches of skin, grew numerous and did not go away. Unable to work, she lay in her room, having night sweats that leeched out precious fluids. Lupe lost weight and a dry, heaving cough exhausted her. The curandera could not heal the mysterious disease.

"You must eat something, Lupe. Here is soup from yesterday. It is still good. Please swallow something. Here is a wet rag for your face. What can I do for you?"

"Stay with me, please."

"After work I will spend the night, but I must go now. I lit a candle for you and in my prayers I have asked la Virginita for help."

Angelita stayed the night with her sister; she could not save her. Lupe slipped away in the early hours of the morning. When it was light enough, Angelita informed Sra. Garcia, who in turn called the priest, who alerted the authorities. Hurriedly, the body was buried with little ceremony the next day in the paupers' field. Sra. Garcia paid the priest and the undertaker, as she had done a hundred times.

Saying her last goodbye at the grave, with tears welling in her eyes, Angelita thought, *Before, I did what Papa and Mama wanted. I want more now.*

Resolutely, she walked away from la zona, clutching her few possessions and her old, corn-husk doll.

LNEAGLE

LUCY'S NEXT TASK

Lucy Mullens glanced at her gnarled, fifty-seven-year old hands. They were used to hard work. Tall, thin, having brown hair, Lucy had seen West Texas change from a rough wilderness to a place with roads and highways.

She and Paul, her husband of forty-one years, had reared two children, who had grown up, married and moved away. Lucy, feeling her life was complete, faced a new chapter dawning in her life.

In her younger days, she had helped Paul homestead and clear the land. She could grub mesquite trees and haul the stumps with a team of horses as well as any man. Married in 1902, Lucy and Paul came to West Texas in a covered wagon. They staked out their land amid rattlesnakes and sandstorms, punctuated by blue Northers in the winter and severe droughts in the summers, with an occasional Comanche who escaped from the reservations in Oklahoma, who came to hunt the few remaining buffalo roaming the country.

"Now, I've got another job to do. I hope I'm up to the task."

Paul had gone to town to meet the train. Their daughter-in-law Eunice was coming home from the tuberculosis sanitarium in San Angelo. On the way home, he was picking up their grandchildren from their other grandparents over in Red Mud. Eunice had gone for the cure, only to be told that there was nothing they could do for her. She was coming home to die.

Willie and Rachel, her children, spent time with both sets of grandparents.

Their father David had volunteered for World War II when war broke out. Now in 1943, he had not been home to see his family in two years. He sent money to help when he could. He didn't feel that he needed a compassionate leave; because Eunice had convinced him she'd be fine when she went to the sanatarium in San Angelo.

Paul met the train, picked up Eunice, and on the way home, got the grandchildren.

Lucy thought, "I'm too old for this task. I'm not sure I can do it. I don't have the strength I used to have to tend the children."

The '37 Ford appeared leading a dust trail in the distance. The country road was muddy when it rained and dusty when dry. Lucy stood, scanning the distance, looking for hope, a purpose, or some idea to help her cope. The car's intrusion into her thoughts jerked her back into reality.

When the old car came to a halt, Lucy stepped off the porch and walked through the oak trees to the edge of the lawn. Opening the car door, she said, "Welcome, Eunice. It is good to see you. How was the trip?"

Straining to be heard, Eunice, pale and thin, spoke slowly and quietly, "It was fine. I am very tired. Maybe we can visit some more after I take a nap."

Lucy looked at Paul, "Get her things out of the car while I'll help her into the guestroom."

Paul said, "I need to put the car in the garage before I start my chores. There is a storm brewing off in the west."

Lucy nodded, "Okay."

Opening the door of the car, Lucy said, "Willie, you take your Mama's suitcase, and Rachel, you open the screen door for us. Be quick, now." The youngsters hurried to do their assignments.

Once in the guest room, Lucy closed the door. She helped Eunice slip into her thin, lacy gown, noticing how frail she was. She had lost a lot of weight.

Biscuits and gravy will put the fat back on her bones, and maybe some pork and beans, too.

With great exertion, Eunice got into the four-poster bed in the spare bedroom. Lucy drew the drapes to keep the hot, afternoon sun from intruding into the dark room. Once Eunice was settled, Lucy stepped out of the room quietly closing the door.

Stepping into the hall, Lucy said, "You kids come with me into the kitchen. We need to be quiet so your Mama can rest. I think there's a slice of watermelon waiting for you."

Nine-year-old Rachel was worried. "Grandma, is Mama going to be all right?"

"I'm not sure, honey."

"Well, she was supposed to stay for nine months for the cure, but she only stayed three months."

"Rachel, I don't know much about your Mama's illness. Nobody does. We'll just have to wait and hope."

Willie, two years younger than Rachel, began to sob. He didn't understand all that was said, but felt the emotions.

"Hush, Willie, now you must be brave for your Mama's sake. Let's go into the kitchen. You still like watermelon, don't you?"

The children were soon distracted by the juicy watermelon.

When they had finished, Lucy said, "Willie, you go see if Grandpa needs some help with his chores. I expect he'll want you to gather the eggs. Watch old Bertha Mae. She's been hiding her eggs in the field."

"Yes, Ma'am."

"Now, Rachel, I want you to throw the rinds in the trash and help me start supper."

Without further comment, the children got up from the table to do as they were asked.

Three weeks later, Eunice was no better. Her will seemed to be the one thing keeping her alive. Paul drove into town to notify the doctor. Doctor Hall said he'd come as soon as he could get away.

Lucy heard the old car as it returned to the old farmhouse. Looking out the screened porch, Lucy saw Paul picking at the cracked paint on the window screens. The old house, well-built when new, showed signs of age. The concrete porch was pulling away from the stucco house.

Paul glanced at Lucy, "Sure does need a new coat of paint."

"Yes, replied Lucy, "It's getting old, just like we are. Lots of wear and tear. When can we expect the doctor?"

"As soon as he can get away, " responded Paul.

Not long after, Dr. Hall's car rumbled up to the front of the house. Opening the door for the doctor, Paul said, "Thanks for coming. Eunice is in the room on the left of the hall."

After his examination, Doctor Hall said, "Eunice, you better get your house in order. The medicine I prescribed isn't doing the job. There is little else I can do, except give you something for the pain."

Eunice nodded. Lucy sensed the diagnosis, even before the doctor had completed his exam.

Lucy muttered under her breath, "Denial is easier when you don't know all the answers." Then, turning to Doctor Hall, she said, "Thanks for coming, Doc. Is there anything I can do?" asked Lucy.

"Keep her quiet and comfortable is about all. I'll check on her one day next week."

Eunice called, "Mother Mullins, I need to speak to you. I love my parents but they can't take care of the kids. You have been so good to us all. Would you see to my children when I'm gone?"

"I wouldn't think of doing anything else. They are David's children, too."

"Thank you for all you've done. I can rest easily now. Would you call the kids for me?"

Lucy, wiping her eyes with the corner of her apron, called Willie to come into the bedroom. Speaking with great difficulty, Eunice said, "Willie. You have always been a good boy. I'm sure you'll grow up to be a fine man. Don't give your Grandma or Grandpa any grief. I expect you to do what you are told and help around the farm."

Willie sat on the bed, holding his mother's hand, and listening to the words. Nodding all the while, tears were streaming down his face. "All right, Mama," he said, sobbing.

"I love you, Willie and I want you to look after your sister. While your Daddy is gone, you are the man she needs to look after her."

"I love you, too, Mama," said Willie. "I'll try."

Lucy led Willie from the room and brought Rachel to her Mother's bed.

"Rachel, I need both of you to look out for each other. Willie is young. He'll need help growing up. I love you and know you'll grow into a beautiful lady. Watch out for yourself, obey your grandparents and take care of Willie."

"All right, Mama, I'll do my best."

Eunice's body slowly wore out. Daily she grew weaker and weaker. Her will left her body as rust works on metal, slowly but completely. The end came at the dawn of a new day, with Lucy at her side.

"For some reason, God gave me these poor little children to care for. I'll do my best."

Eunice was buried in the grove of trees on the far side of the pasture. With little ceremony, she was, at last, at peace.

Lucy, despite her age, with Paul's help, reared the young ones. Lucy was seventy-two when Rachel graduated from nursing school; she was seventy-eight when Willie graduated from law school.

A GOOD MAN TO KNOW

Soapy Moore, the old bachelor deputy sheriff, came by Consumers' Gas Station every day in order to visit Eva Nell Smith, the cashier. Soapy, well past thirty, had begun to develop a middle-age paunch. The belt around his Wranglers continued to fall below his stomach, as he insisted on buying the same size blue jeans. Keeping his belt size the same, created, for him, the illusion that his physical appearance had not changed. He had a pleasant smile, because his job was political, brown eyes and thinning, brown hair.

Soapy had a widowed, invalid mother whose care had been his responsibility for the past fifteen years. While she was not demanding of Soapy, his mother did require attention, which took all his spare time. While he was on duty, she had a neighbor seeing after her, and she knew not to bother him. Since the job was mostly hanging around the coffee shop for something to happen, he had enough time to spend with Eva Nell.

Eva Nell Smith was the oldest daughter of Elijah Smith, the owner of the gas station. Tall and thin, she had missed several opportunities at marriage, but she'd read too many magazines about the lives of adventurous movie stars to settle for a farmer, a teacher, or the undertaker. Soapy hoped she might eventually settle for a deputy sheriff, her knight in shining armor.

Staring out the window between customers, Eva mused, "Soapy must have a wonderful life chasing bank robbers from Lubbock, or rescuing women from raging floods."

While the reality of Soapy's life was vastly different from Eva Nell's perception, he did little to discourage her crush. More often than he liked, he got the widow Jones' cat out of a tree, or he helped Uncle Joe Thornton change a flat tire.

Lately, he had moved his 'office' from the Good Eats Cafe to Consumers', just to spend time with Eva. Mr. Smith, Eva's father, knew what Soapy was up to, having been a young man fifty years ago. He approved of the courtship, though he probably would approve of any man that would marry his daughter, especially since she still lived at home and read *True Romance* magazine. A constant irritation to her father was that Eva Nell delighted in retelling all the plots of the characters at mealtime.

∞∞∞

Built in 1920, Consumers' Service Station had changed little in the ensuing thirty years. The customers pumped their own gasoline using the original fixtures, which consisted of gazing up at the glass container, attempting to read the marks, while pumping the gas. Though inaccurate, the procedure remained for lack of any new innovations.

Inside the station, the original slab, concrete flooring was unchanged since it was initially poured. A large pot-bellied butane stove, surrounded by wooden chairs, held a prominent space. Most of the farmers who came to town on Saturday gathered around the stove while their wives shopped at the local merchants.

"Have you seen any of the new pictures of wanted men around here lately, Soapy?" asked Eva Nell. "The post office has just put some up."

"No, but there was a strange fellow hanging around Clem Parson's tractor while I was driving around this morning. As soon as he saw me, he took off. I'm still watching for him."

Walking into the station, Mr. Stewart reached into his pocket to pay for the gas. His son Tommy was following. "How are you Eva Nell? Just as pretty as always."

"Thank you, Mr. Stewart. Would that be all, or did you want something else?"

"Yes, I would like a couple of sacks of Bull Durham."
Looking at Tommy, he continued, "Do you see a candy bar
you want?"

"Could I have a Butterfinger?" said Tommy pointing at
the glass case by the register.

Reaching down for the candy bar, Eva placed the
tobacco and the candy bar on the counter and totaled the
bill.

Mr. Stewart counted out the bills and handed them to
Eva, who placed the money in the register. "Thank you and
be sure to come back." Looking at Tom she said, "Now,
Tom, don't you be a stranger. I know a lot of girls who think
you are cute as a button."

Ten-year-old Tom blushed and smiled as he chomped
down on his candy bar. He hurried to catch up with his
father who was walking toward the door. Soapy, standing
back so Mr. Stewart could pay his bill, stepped into Eva's
line-of-sight.

"What are you doing tonight after work?" asked Eva
frowning.

"I hope I can get Mable to stay with Mama so we can
go to the movies. Is that what you want?"

Looking up from the cash register, she said, "It would
be nice if you asked me, instead of waiting until the last
minute."

"I thought you understood about my work and Mama
and all."

"I do, but some time I may say 'no' just to teach you
a lesson. Clark Gable would never do Vivian Leigh that
way."

"I'm sorry. Will you go with me tonight to see Tom Mix bring justice to the old west?"

Smiling, she said, "Yes. Pick me up at eight, or call me if there is a jail break at Guthrie and you can't go."

Nodding, Soapy turned to walk outside, when the explosion occurred. The building erupted, with large pieces of concrete being blown into the air. The tin roof looked like a flying carpet above the debris. The supporting wooden beams broke like toothpicks between two fingers. Dirt, dust, concrete, and tin formed a picture of a smoking bomb crater. What could burn, did.

Over time, the butane stove had developed a small leak. The gas slowly sank beneath the concrete floor of the station, collecting into a dangerous pool. A spark from a tossed cigarette ignited the blast. The flames co-mingled with the dust.

Immediately after the explosion, Soapy was thrown toward the door. Sensing what had happened, he grabbed Mr. Stewart and pushed him outside. Returning to the store, he quickly found Eva, who was unconscious. He dragged her from the conflagration. As soon as she was safely outside, Soapy returned to look for Tommy and Mr. Smith, who was in the back of the store checking on his tire inventory.

Recalling the approximate location of the cash stand, Soapy glanced through the smoke and dust looking for Tommy. With no moment to spare, Soapy tripped over Tommy's feet, sticking out from behind the remains of the counter. Quickly Soapy dragged Tommy outside to flashing lights and sirens. The volunteer fire department arrived, but the heat and the smoke made further attempts at rescue impossible.

Seeing Joe Bob step from the fire truck, Soapy motioned rapidly. "Joe Bob, get over here. Tommy is coming around, but I need to find Mr. Smith. You tend to Tommy."

Joe Bob Scott shouted above the noise and confusion, "Soapy, you can't go in there. The fire is too hot and the smoke is too thick. Besides, you're hurt. Are you sure there are others inside?"

Nodding and reaching up to check the blood on his forehead, surprised, Soapy added, "Yes, Mr. Smith was in the back of the store. Tell your crew to try the back entrance and maybe you can find him."

The volunteer firemen did not wait for orders but ran around the inferno towards the back of the station.

Looking around after catching his breath, Soapy said, "How is Eva?"

"The ambulance carried her and Mr. Stewart to the hospital, " said Joe Bob. "You need to get that gash on your head attended to. Go on to the hospital. The sheriff called and is on his way here. He can take charge."

"Well, I can't do much now." Trying to stop the bleeding, Soapy glanced at Joe Bob. "I'm going to check on Eva Nell. Tell the sheriff where I've gone."

Arriving at the hospital, Soapy hurried to the emergency room. "How is Eva?" he asked the attending nurse.

"She'll be fine. She got a pretty good lick on her head, but is awake now. There doesn't appear to be any permanent damage."

"When can I see her?" asked Soapy.

"Right after we examine that gash on your head."

Seven stitches later, Soapy wanted to see Eva. By this time she had been transferred to a room.

"How are you, Eva?"

"I ache, but I am fine. The doctor wants to keep me overnight for observation. How is daddy?"

"We don't know yet. The last time I saw him he was going to the back of the store to check on a tractor tire for Mr. Williams."

While Soapy and Eva were talking, the ambulance brought Mr. Smith to the emergency room. Hearing the commotion, Soapy stepped out of the room.

"Hank, how is Mr. Smith?"

"He is dazed, but appears to be fine. The initial blast knocked him into the alley. We didn't see him till he got up and started walking around. The doctor wants to be sure, though."

"Thanks, Hank, I'll tell Eva Nell," Soapy said as he returned to her room.

"I guess I won't be able to make the movie tonight," she said.

"That's all right. I plan to spend my time at the hospital holding your hand."

THE FINAL STRAW

Sitting at his desk, Professor William Nall looked up from a leather chair that was too large for his small frame. His gray temples and thin, bony fingers reminded students of a bantam rooster that picks a fight with anything or anyone in his domain. Dr. Nall tossed Charles Fox's thesis aside with a sneer.

"Before I came to Lubbock, I was the academic dean in a university in Iowa. Since I took this appointment at the university, I've seen nothing but unacceptable work. I'm convinced west Texas students are inferior to students in other schools."

Scratching his head, Charles Fox replied, "Well, Dr. Nall, I guess that's probably true, but they slipped up and gave me a degree Magna Cum Laude at the University of Texas when I graduated in 1960. I guess they didn't get the word from you."

Glancing up quickly with a smirk on his face, Dr. Nall replied, "Don't be impertinent with me. Not if you intend to finish this Master's Degree."

Shrugging his shoulders, Charles said, "Professor Nall, what do you want from me? I didn't intend to offend, it's just that so much is riding on this degree. I've been going to night school for the past four years and have been teaching full time. I need this degree to get a better job."

Like a boxer winning a fight, Dr. Nall said, "I expect a change in your attitude by the next appointment." Checking his calendar, he looked at Charles. "With the Christmas break you have just over three weeks before we return for classes in January. I expect you to rewrite the summary and make a new outline. Start over. I don't like anything you've written to date. After I have finished reading your revisions, I'll make up my mind about you."

Walking down the stairs, taking time to spit the sand out of his mouth, Charles reflected:

The holidays could not come at a worse time. I don't know why that pompous ass talks to me that way. He gets away with it because he controls whether I graduate or not. It's too late to find another thesis director. I'm really tired of the school kids and while I don't hate Guthrie, or the community, it's just a dead-end job. There's got to be more to life than that.

Facing a cold, bitter December sandstorm as he walked across campus, Charles heard his buddy, Joe Ray calling him.

"Hey, Chuck. Why the gloomy look?"

"I just had a talk with Dr. Nall. He threatened me again and said I couldn't finish the degree. I don't know what I'm going to do."

"So, what's the worse thing that could happen to you?"

"You don't understand. I need this degree. It would get me out of the Guthrie schools and into a good school, like Lubbock. Without it I'm stuck in a rural, one-horse school and poverty. I want something better than that."

Changing the subject, Joe Ray asked, "What are you doing for Christmas?"

"Looks like I'm rewriting my thesis and I'll go to Tahoka to visit my Mom."

"Well, my friend Carl Aaron and I are going to Mexico City for the week of Christmas. Why don't you come along? The trip would do you good and when you divide the cost by three, it will be pretty cheap. Besides, one week, more or less, won't hurt the rewrite. The change of scenery might even do you some good."

"Do you think Carl would mind? I don't know him."

"I met him in physics class last year. He's from Idalou. I don't see why he would object."

"Well, ask him. If he agrees, then I'll go. If he says no, then I'll just hang out around home."

"I'll see him for a final in English on Thursday. I'll drop by your house when I come home to Guthrie on Friday."

"Thanks, see you then."

On Friday, Joe Ray stopped by Chuck's apartment. "He said okay. The only problem is he drinks heavily, and doesn't want his Baptist friends to know about it. I assured him that not only do we drink, but we can keep a secret."

"Good. What are the plans?"

"We'll go by Idalou and pick Carl up on Monday. It will take us all day to drive to El Paso. We'll put my car in storage, walk across the International Bridge, and catch the train in Cuidad Juarez. We can get our tourist cards on the border and board the train in a couple of hours."

"It sounds like you have done some planning. I can't wait. What time do you want to come by for me?"

"I'll be by at seven. That way, if we have car trouble, we'll have plenty of time to fix it and still make the train."

"Fine. Thanks for asking me to go. This trip is going to be more fun than visiting my family. I'll see you early the morning of the twentieth."

"Okay, I've got to go home, do a load of clothes, and pack. See you soon."

The next thing Chuck needed to do was dial his mother in Tahoka. "Hello, mom. How are you?"

Fumbling with the knots of the phone cord, "Yes, this is Charles. Listen, Mom, I'm going to Mexico City over Christmas. I'm going with Joe Ray and another friend. I'll have to mail my presents to you and the family to your house."

Shifting his weight from the right to the left leg, he continued, "Yes, ma'am, I'm sure I want to go. No, I'm not mad at anyone, especially cousin Wanda Fay. No, there are no girls involved, I simply need to get away. I promise you I'll spend time with you when I return. Please understand. I love you, bye."

That was easier than I thought it would be.

Waiting in line at the post office, Chuck spoke briefly to Mrs. Williams. "Yes, Mrs. Williams, I think Virginia Ruth is a very smart young lady. You've done a good job raising her. Have a Merry Christmas." *For ten whole days, I won't have to see a single parent or a spoiled child. What a relief.* Stepping up to the window, he replied, "Yes, Clarence, I've got a lot of packages going to Tahoka. No, I'm not taking them this year. Thanks."

On the morning appointed, Joe Ray honked the horn of his '67 Dodge Charger. The car was five years' old, but dependable. Chuck grabbed his suitcase and turned to lock the door of his apartment.

Joe Ray spoke first, "Good morning, Chuck. I see you're traveling light. It's supposed to be ninety-five degrees while we are there."

Peeling rubber like a teenager, Joe Ray pressed the accelerator. The Charger obeyed; in fact, he had numerous speeding tickets to prove the car's performance. Arriving in Idalou, Carl quickly loaded his clothes and the trio headed for El Paso. En route, they experienced a sand storm, a rain shower, and the remnants of the cold front that passed through the panhandle earlier last week.

Nothing could dampen their spirits; three explorers were on their way to adventure.

Upon arriving, they found the parking garage. The group embarked and made their way across the bridge linking the two countries.

The police station, adjacent to the railroad was easy to find. After filling out the necessary forms and getting their tourist visas, they spotted a large restaurant with an enormous, glitzy, neon sign, announcing that it specialized in *cabrito.*

Having drowned the barbecued goat with numerous drinks, no one could vouch for the food's quality. The sunlight was fading as they boarded the train. The entire process of eating, getting tourist cards, and parking the car took less than two hours.

After finding the compartment, Joe Ray asked the conductor, "*Senor, donde esta la cantina?*"

"The bar is in the next car."

"Thanks. Come on fellows, let's see what they have to drink."

The monotonous trip was punctuated by sudden, unexpected stops. The desert was best experienced at night. With little to see but endless miles of desert, the boys spent their time drinking while the distant mountains loomed nearer in the darkness.

The train suddenly lurched, spilling Joe Ray's drink on himself. "Why are we stopping here? I know we aren't there yet."

"No," said another passenger, "The train is the only transportation in the desert. At certain points, the train stops for boarding and unloading."

As soon as he'd finished talking, the trio saw men and women with their children and bundles getting on the train. Just as suddenly, the train lurched forward, as if arguing with the rails to permit its departure.

Stopping in the small towns en route, the passengers witnessed the bright lights and Christmas decorations announcing the coming holiday. The following morning, the desert faded into low hills, which grew larger, and eventually became mountains. The locomotive was climbing.

Joe Ray said, "Man, what did I drink last night?"

"I don't think it was what you drank, but how much," said Carl, picking his teeth with a credit card. "I don't think my teeth have ever itched before."

"I think they put something in the drinks. The Mexican beer didn't seem to have much kick," said Chuck.

"After several margaritas, some shots of tequila, and then several cans of beer, maybe that's why you have an upset stomach." said Joe Ray.

Carl replied, "It's not my stomach, it's my head. It feels like a jack hammer is inside breaking concrete."

In no shape for sight-seeing that evening, as soon as they found their rooms, "good nights" were exchanged and the adventurers disappeared.

The first floor of the Hotel Metropole contained a small bar and a restaurant. The next morning, reading brochures, the three waited for their breakfasts.

Having too much to see in the time allowed, the trio spent their days visiting as many sites as they could: Chapultec Castle, the National Museum, the pyramids, and the bullfights. The nights were spent drinking, dancing, and walking in the Reforma Park watching the people. Because it was Christmas, the parents wanted their children's picture with a bearded Wise man, who terrified the younger ones.

On the day before Christmas, the men went to the famous floating gardens of Xochimilco.

"I had no idea the weather would be this hot, especially at Christmas." said Joe Ray. "We are up in the mountains here and it's at least 95 degrees."

LHEAGLE

Chuck said, "We are used to West Texas. It is cool at home at Christmas; here the air is thin and warm. Enjoy. The Aztecs enjoyed these floating gardens with all the flowers just like we are."

After a full day of sun and sight-seeing, Carl said, "As soon as I get to the hotel, I'm going to take a hot shower and go to bed."

Joe Ray agreed, "This weather and this trip are wearing me out. I think I'll turn in early, too."

Chuck answered, "I'm not ready to call it a day yet. I want another drink."

Walking into the hotel bar, Chuck spoke quietly, "One cervesa, por favor."

"You are American, right?" asked Juan, the waiter.

"Yeah, Texan," said Chuck.

"I went to the United States for graduate study a couple of years' ago."

Why am I having this conversation? I took this trip to get away from school and pompous professors. Now I have to listen to this drivel from a Mexican I don't know, nor care to know. I wish he'd shut up and let me drink quietly.

"I went to Parson's College in Iowa. Do you know the school?"

"No, can't say as I do."

"Well, I hated the place. The academic dean did nothing to help the students. When the students fail out of Ivy League schools, their parents enroll them at Parson's College. They really need help or they wouldn't be there. All Dr. Nall did was remain in his office and write books, so he could get a better job. He did nothing to help anyone but himself. I got disgusted and left. There have to be better schools and better people than there."

"Did you say his name was Dr. Nall?"

"Si, William Nall. I think he went some place in Texas."

A tidal wave of awareness washed over Chuck's consciousness. "He went to Tech at Lubbock. I know him, and I agree with your description. He still isn't helping students. He thinks he is superior because of his teaching position."

"Well, I quit grad school because of him and came home. I'm bar tending between semesters. I attend the University of Mexico City now."

— The Final Straw —

Chuck studied the beads of sweat on the beer can. He felt a key unlocking a mystery he had not verbalized. Now, the tumblers aligned, falling into place somewhere in his mind. Unlocking the door, the Nall enigma was complete.

"Thank you."

I've got you, Nall. I know what you are. I know where you're from. And I don't quit. You are no better than I am.

"Could I buy you a drink, Amigo? You've made my day."

SUNDOWN

Preacher Bob hunkered down on the running board of his old Model T. Ford, trying to get comfortable. Salty sweat beaded on his eyebrows, then flowed downward, stinging his eyes. His white, starched collar had lost its crisp freshness, as had his Sunday shirt. From time to time, Bob glanced at the depot wall, grumbling to himself as the clock's progress reduced his respite between morning and evening services.

Damned, Texas summer.

Wiping his eyelids with his sleeve, he counted three sand devils, stirring paths through the stunted, dry cotton stalks.

How could the cotton withstand the onslaught?

The preacher cast his mind back to 1928 to his arrival in Dickens. Back then, the town wore a coat of paint, people milled around, shopping and talking with an air of expectancy. Stepping down from the train, he had hoped to feel at home and fulfill the promises he'd made to Lucy.

None of that had happened: No one expected the Dust Bowl to occur, nor the crops to fail. No one expected the bank to repossess the land nor the need for folks to move away to find work. The congregation could not meet his salary, and the parsonage fell into perpetual disrepair.

Lucy's complaints echoed in his ear: "Why do I have to go to church all the time and live up to the expectations of those ladies in the guild?"

Lucy never grew comfortable in the role as a minister's wife. "Why do I have to be an example to the congregation and be so careful about what I say and when I say it? Why don't you try to get work, since we can't live on the salary you get?"

After two years, Lucy resigned from her unofficial post and the marriage; she and Beth escaped on the train.

Everything she said was true. Even my sermons are stolen from journals. I can't seem to think of anything to say.

His life in Dickens imitated the cotton stalks, dusty, dry, and stunted. The wind whipped the sand about his feet. Time drove his dreams through the fingers of his rough, cracked hands as it tore through the cotton stalks.

Why did I end up in West Texas? Bad luck and wrong decisions. I had gotten Lucy in a family way. One time in the back of a car, and my education ended.

Leaving seminary without a degree meant migrating from one small church to another for the rest of his pastoral life. No need to apply to more affluent churches.

Lucy and Bob, and now Beth. It didn't matter, that was not enough reason for them to stay together. And the money was never enough. The smaller churches can't pay much so a divorced preacher, while not desirable, was permitted.

Nothing good ever came on the train. The train brought me to this parched country; the train took Lucy and Beth away. Now it is bringing me a pauper to bury.

With more diesels on the tracks, fewer and fewer trains stopped for water. For decades, Dickens had retained value as the water stop between El Paso and Fort Worth for the steam engines. Now, the Dust Bowl had dissipated even the trains.

With no rain, no crops. With no crops, no income. With no income, no dreams.

He glanced around. All he saw was a funeral parlor, a blacksmith shop, and a general store: the picked bones of a ghost town.

The station clock measured by degrees the day's monotony. At five after one, he could see the outline of the steam engine approaching, pulling the train. He stepped across the street to alert John Campbell, the undertaker. Before speaking, he spit to force the dry dust out of his mouth.

Who could overcome the sand, wind, or heat? he thought.

"John, it's time to bring the hearse to the dock."

"Let me get my harnesses. I should be there before the train stops."

"Fine, I'll meet you at the freight door."

At roughly the same time that the train coughed to a halt, the hearse eased alongside the train car. The horses, matched bays with white stockings, were a throwback to an earlier time. Mr. Campbell, like the horses, was living out his last days with as few changes as possible.

The boxcar door gradually opened, revealing the large, cheap wooden box inside. It was time to do his duty.

Why send the body to be buried here? They can afford the ticket home, but not a funeral.

While Bob mused, a starkly, lean boy in his early twenties, stepped next to the casket. The boy seemed world-weary. He looked tired, more tired than a long trip made him. His clean overalls were wrinkled from the trip. His faded, patched shirt was of an indefinite color. His worn boots showed too many days of hard use. The dirty felt hat with a greasy sweat ring around the brim bore silent testimony to hard, manual labor.

The boy approached him, "I'm Tom. Tom Richey. This here's my pa," he said, pointing to the casket.

Bob responded with minimal introductions. "Did you have any trouble on the trip?"

"No, sir. It's just a long way from Fort Worth."

"Tom, when I first settled here, I met a family of Richeys who lived eight miles out on the Jayton road. Are you any kin?"

"Yes, that was my pa's brother. The whole family is gone now. They followed us to Fort Worth about five years ago. My pa is the last one of the family, except for two cousins and me."

"They were a hard-working lot, but they had rotten luck."

Four strangers, standing by the mail drop door, aided by Campbell, carefully placed the casket into the hearse. Campbell thanked the men for their help and motioned for Bob to get up on the seat next to him. He declined.

LNEAGLE

"No, I will walk with Tom."

John snapped the reins and the horses responded. The pitiful company moved slowly toward its destination, the sand dogging the wagon wheels and slipping into the men's shoes.

They did not talk. With each step Bob and Tom took, the persistent dust stirred up.

Breaking the silence, Tom said, "This is hard, but I am going to finish it. I promised Pa."

The gravediggers were completing their job as the group approached. John nodded at the men who climbed out of the grave, opened the hearse, and gently lowered the casket into the open grave.

"Thank you for being my pa's pall bearers," Tom said, not knowing they would be paid.

The gravediggers' faded clothes resembled the mourner's, except for the grime.

Suddenly, Tom felt the desolation: the open grave, the wooden casket, the long trip, and the strangers burying Pa. He stood quietly, hat-in-hand, with his head bowed.

"Dearly beloved," Bob began his standard funeral speech. "We are gathered today in the sight of God to send the soul of Isaiah Richey on its way to heaven."

Bob had given his speech so many times that it sounded to him like rote. Not knowing the deceased, nor the young man personally, Bob still wanted to reassure Tom.

"While I never met Isaiah, I know the family. Without fail, the Richeys worked hard, were honest, and helped their neighbors when called upon. Like most farmers, they taught their kids right from wrong."

Bob closed the brief service with some verses of scripture.

After the Lord's Prayer, Bob nodded to John, who signaled the men to close the grave. Bob put his hand to Tom's shoulder and led him away, knowing that the undertaker would wait until the grave was closed, then pay the men and return to town.

With tears on his face, Tom said, "I wish it had not happened this way. The county paid for the burial. Pa ended up in the Potter's Field."

Silence followed and then Tom removed a coin from his pocket. "Preacher, this silver dollar is all I have. I want you to take it."

"Don't you need this more than I do, son?"

"It's all I can do for Pa or for you." Tom sobbed, "Besides, I have a return ticket and the promise of a job when I get home."

Reluctantly, Bob took the coin, slipping it in his coat pocket. Bob and Tom nodded to each other, slowly turning and walking back to town, each keeping his own counsel.

UNCLE EUGENE'S HELP

Caroline stepped across the kitchen and separated the curtain, looking out on the barns, the cotton field, and the clouds. The cows were unusually restive, but she figured their nervousness was because milking time was near. Already she had spread the cold cuts and vegetables on the table for anyone who wanted to eat. The family had come from church and had spent the afternoon, taking turns visiting with Amanda, Bob's mother, and cooling off on the front porch. The day had been marked by stifling June heat, with little relief in sight. No one was surprised: it was summer in Texas.

"Bob," said Caroline, "what are we going to do about your mother?"

Robert looked at her quizzically, "What do you mean? Doctor Hale has already said that he's done all he can do."

"Have you noticed the weather? We are in for some severe changes as sure as can be. Something has to break this heat spell we are in. I believe we are going to have a hail storm, or a tornado, or something worse."

"You may be right, but I don't see how this affects Mama," said Bob.

"Well, she's not well enough to be carried to the storm cellar, if we have to go."

"I guess someone will have to stay with her then," said Bob.

"I don't think you should be the one. We've taken care of her since the accident. I don't mind, but I think one of your brothers or sisters should help out. They have done precious little to help out," said Caroline.

As the couple got older, Amanda and George moved into a smaller house in town, selling the home place to Bob. In a few years, following the natural progression of time, George passed away. Shortly after the funeral, Bob, as the oldest child, called the family together.

With Dad gone, it's clear that Mama can't take care of herself. She depended on Dad for everything. I'm not sure how much help I will get from the others, but we need to talk about Mama.

As the oldest, it was Bob's responsibility to officiate at the gathering. "We are here to talk about Mama. For certain, she will have a hard time living alone, since Dad looked after her like a mother cat with a kitten. The question is: where will she live?"

Breaking the silence, Mary Lou, Bob's baby sister, spoke before anyone else could. She had met and married Al, a man from up North someplace and lived in a small apartment in town. Mary Lou whined to all who would listen about how sorry her husband was. In fact, Mary Lou enjoyed her complaining more than an alcoholic's wife at the AA support groups.

"Bob, I simply can't take Mama. The apartment is too small, besides I have social obligations. I have a bridge club that meets each Wednesday, and she simply would not fit in. You understand, don't you?"

"Yes," said Bob. *I am not surprised. As the baby, she has always thought of herself first. I'd pity anybody who had to live with her.*

"Edith Anne, could you take Mama?"

"I could, Bob, but with two teenagers coming and going all the time, it would be hard. The kids wouldn't mind their grandma, but she would never have any peace and quiet. There's not a place in the house where anyone can go to be quiet. Cindy has joined the band and is practicing the saxophone. I hope we live through it."

She makes complete sense. While Mama would enjoy the activities of young people, she does enjoy her quiet.

"Let's go around the group before deciding anything final." said Bob.

"Homer," said Bob, "Would you agree to take care of Mama?"

"I'd be happy to, but you know that Thelma Jean and Mama fight like Gen. McArthur and Harry Truman. I'm afraid no one would be happy in this arrangement."

I think Mama would win the war, but it would wear her down after awhile.

"Eugene, you've been awfully quiet. Would you take Mama in?"

"Bob, you know I would, but I am at work most days and Mama would be lonely. She doesn't know anyone at Crosbyton and when I come home, I sometimes like a drink. Mama would be on my case the entire time. Besides, a little drink makes me feel good. I've got a bottle in the car, if you want a drink."

Mary Lou jumped into the discussion before anyone else could speak. "You sorry skunk, I'm ashamed you belong to this family. When I think of Papa and Mama and their standing in the community and the Methodist Church, I could stay embarrassed at the things you do. Bob, I don't want Mama living with Eugene. He was born drunk and has never drawn a sober breath since then."

Eugene could not help but hear and shrugged his shoulders, "Mary Lou, I've got needs. Drink helps me live with them. I wish you'd understand. I don't ever get drunk, only happy."

Mary Lou sat very still and scowled like a child that had gotten a taste of vinegar by mistake. For sure, she'd be praying for the besotted sinner at the Wesleyan Service Guild on Tuesday.

I wish she'd stay on the subject. I expect she'll criticize the devil when she goes to hell.

Elmer Dee was the last one to speak, "Ever since Alma ran off with that school teacher and moved to Lubbock to discover the meaning of life, I have been dating. Some of my lady friends are nice, but Mama would not like them. Besides, she would cramp my style."

Finally, it occurred to the group to ask their mother. When Amanda walked into the room, she expressed her desires. She wanted to live out her days in the old home place. Bob, her eldest, agreed and Caroline made the best of the situation. She loved Amanda dearly, but two women in the same house were like two territorial Bantam roosters.

While Amanda was fully twenty years older than Caroline, she made an effort to defer to her when she could. Caroline, in turn, asked for suggestions and ideas.

The problem arose when Caroline wanted to fight with Bob. His mother always took his side in any argument. In order to say what she felt, Carolina had to follow Bob out to the barn and tell him what she wanted. She made many trips out to the barn to speak her mind.

"Why did you go into town with your mother and forget to buy that bolt of domestic cloth for me?"

"Well," said Bob, "Mama needed help in getting her medicine and some other things. We ran out of time. I'm sorry."

"Not half as sorry as you should be. I've been out of ticking for the new mattress for weeks. I've got the goose feathers collected, but I can't make the mattress until you get off your rear end and pay attention to my needs, too."

As good-natured as Bob was, he had married a woman with his mother's temperament. Both women were hardheaded and determined to make Bob behave, even if it might kill him, but Bob usually smiled and ignored both of them. He often knew he was in trouble, but he knew the trouble would pass.

Not long after moving into the old guest room, Amanda decided to prove that she could do as much work, as she had thirty years ago. Amanda had milked the cows when she and George had first started their life together. She decided that she could help out by milking again. Both Caroline and Bob protested, but nothing could dissuade her.

One evening, Bob glanced up to see his mother's cheek bleeding. "Mama, what's wrong?" asked Bob who was in the kitchen bringing water from the well.

"The spring that's attached to the gate in the feed lot snapped and hit me in the cheek. It is bleeding a lot, but it doesn't hurt much."

"Well, maybe you should rest a few days and l will do the milking," said Bob.

Toward the end of the month, Bob needed to take the womenfolk to town.

Carolina was not about to trust Bob with her list. While they were getting out of the car, Dr. Hale, who had an office in the back of the Diamond Drug, walked out front.

"Miss Amanda, what have you gotten yourself into?"

"Oh, the spring on the barn gate came loose and popped me in the cheek."

"You better let me take a look at it. It could become serious."

"If I have enough time, I will." said Amanda.

"Bob," said the Dr. "You bring her by, for sure."

After a brief examination, Dr. Hale's suspicions were accurate. "Amanda, the tear on your cheek caused a growth to start. It is cancer and in 1944 we have no treatment for it. I could cut it out, but it would simply return."

Amanda argued with the doctor's diagnosis, but the area continued to be angry and increased in size. Two years passed before Amanda's condition became critical. Carolina nursed her and kept her quiet, but the family had gathered for the end.

After church, Dr. Hale had driven out to the farmhouse, expressing comfort, but knowing there was little he could do. He expressed his sorrow to the children and gave Amanda some sleeping pills to ease the pain.

All of a sudden, the wind calmed, as if to regain strength, and began blowing with greater intensity. The sky darkened and the roar of the approaching storm became evident. The elements had to be reckoned with, and soon.

"Bob, what are we going to do about your mother?"

"Caroline, I don't think it is a problem yet."

"Bob, the storm is getting closer. I expect we are in for a bad hailstorm, or a tornado. How will we get her into the storm cellar? She's in a lot of pain and it would hurt her to move her."

Slowly Bob paid attention and scratched his head, "Well, if we can't move Mama, then someone will have to stay with her, while the rest of us go to the cellar."

As they looked out the bedroom window at the clouds, both of them saw Eugene taking a sack out of the car and tilting the contents to his lips.

Startled by the sounds of the wind, the rest of the family moved toward the window and looked at the scene.

Elmer Dee, the self-appointed group spokesman, said, "I don't think that God intends for all of us to be killed if the tornado comes out of those clouds. Maybe one of us should stay with Mama, while the rest of us save ourselves."

Edith Anne, Homer and Elmer Dee nodded in agreement. As soon as Eugene walked into the house, Mary Lou spoke, "Eugene, Mama has been calling for you. Why don't you go in and visit with her while we watch the clouds?"

LNEAGLE

— Uncle Eugene's Help —

Happily, Eugene scooted his chair over to the bed and started talking. Unbeknownst to Eugene, Amelia was fast asleep.

The storm raged, the sand blew with a vengeance, the rain came in sheets, and the tornado blew past, striking within two hundred yards of the house. While the cotton crop suffered, because the storm was in an open area, little damage was done.

After thirty minutes or so, the family returned from the cellar to find Eugene still talking to Mama totally unaware of his surroundings and his heroic act.

——— ∞∞∞ ———

SHERIFF BILLY'S PLAN

William Leroy Chastain, also known as Billy, woke up that morning remembering the award he was to receive. He was of average height, with brown hair and eyes. Having lived beyond middle age, Buddy had a paunch that hung over his belt buckle. Billy felt the sheriff's star on his chest defrayed anyone's glancing at his enormous belly.

Today, Billy was going to Claremont, as were all the peace officers in the adjoining three counties for a day of fellowship, barbecue, and shooting contests. Every year, the various members of the peace officers in the counties selected one of their own to recognize. Billy was to be singled out for catching three bank robbers, quite by accident, escaping from Rotan.

"Thelma Lou, get up and fix me some breakfast. I'm going to have my picture taken today and I want to look well fed and contented."

"I expect you could go for three weeks and still look fat as a hog."

"Now, Thelma, hush up. I'm going to be recognized by a jury of my peers."

⚬⚬⚬

Answering the phone, Thelma said, "No, Sheriff Chastain is not here. He's gone to Claremont to the Peace Officers Association Meeting. If it is an emergency, call the jail house in Dickens and the deputy can reach him on the radio."

Cleatus Green, the deputy, had also gone to Claremont for the day. No one answered the phone. When the day's events were over, Billy turned on his car radio to discover several missed calls.

"Hello, Jimmy, this is Billy. What seems to be the problem?"

Jimmy Smith, a local car dealer, usually knew the pulse of the county or what the trouble was.

"Well, sheriff, Robert Earl Turner called Joe Bob Bronson and threatened to kill him. Joe Bob came to town and tried to find someone to protect him. All the law officers were in Claremont: no constable, justice of the peace, nor highway patrol could be found. It's as though Robert Earl picked a day when everyone was out of town to get Joe Bob."

"What happened?"

"As soon as Joe Bob saw Robert Earl's pickup, he ran to his and started driving like a crazy person. He left Spur headed for Dickens like a turpentined cat. The problem was that he ran out of gas before he got halfway. Robert Earl shot him as he ran from his pickup."

"Okay, I'll get right on the case. Thanks for the information."

Turning on the red lights, Billy sped as quickly as possible to the scene.

Upon arriving, Billy saw Joe Bob's pickup door standing open with footprints in the field. It appeared that Joe Bob started running and someone took a rifle and killed him. The body was discovered two hundred yards from the highway.

Reaching for the radio, Billy said, "David, this is Billy. There's been a shooting on the Dickens highway and I need you to come and pick up the body."

"Whose body is it?" asked the undertaker.

"It's Joe Bob Bronson. He was shot in the back with a deer rifle."

"All right, sheriff. I'll be there a quickly as I can."

"Thanks, David," said Billy.

Looking at his wristwatch, Billy calculated that Cleatus had gotten back to Dickens and was at the jailhouse. Dialing the number, Billy waited for him to answer the phone. After letting it ring ten times, Cleatus finally answered the call.

"Hello," said Cleatus. "Sheriff's office."

"Cleatus, what's going on? What took you so long to answer the phone?"

"Sheriff, I was afraid."

"Explain yourself."

"I got here about thirty minutes ago. Dorothy got tired of the phone ringing and answered it, after she got her housework done."

"Well?" asked the sheriff.

"It seems that Robert Earl Turner had been calling since the shootout and wanted us to know that he had done it."

"What were you afraid of?"

"Robert Earl said not to come after him, or he'd kill us, too. He also said that he'd come to Dickens and turn himself in when he got good and ready. Sheriff, I say we leave him alone. He's the meanest, toughest bootlegger in these parts and I don't want to mess with him."

"Calm down, Cleatus. Did he say why he shot Joe Bob?"

"No, but the rumor is that his wife was seeing Joe Bob and he was getting revenge."

"Mrs. Turner isn't that attractive, is she? I don't think I know the woman."

"Sheriff, the word is that you don't have to be pretty, if you're available."

"Well, Joe Bob sure picked the wrong woman to get sweet on," said Billy.

"I want you to call the constable, the justice of the peace, and the highway patrol. We've got to pick him up."

"Now, Billy, I wish you'd think about this before acting. All of us are elected officials, except Donald Gene, the highway patrolman. He's the only one mean enough for the job. Let's let sleeping dogs lie."

"Cleatus, by the time I get to Dickens, you'd better be on the phone organizing our posse."

"All right, sheriff, but I'm not inclined to go. Besides, I think it will be dangerous."

Billy hung up the phone. Murder was something new to his county. Occasionally, a drunk would cause trouble or a teenager would get caught speeding, but, by and large, it was a pretty quiet county. Now he had to earn his money by doing his duty, with or without his deputy.

Walking into the jailhouse, Billy noticed that Cleatus was on the phone, as he expected. Glancing through the connecting hallway, he smelled the bologna that Dorothy was frying in the kitchen annex. The jail provided living quarters for the deputy, provided his wife would cook for the inmates. Dorothy made good biscuits and gravy, fried bologna sandwiches and egg salad sandwiches. The prisoners knew better than to complain, and Cleatus didn't know there were other menu options.

Glancing up, Cleatus handed the phone to Billy. "It's Tom Watson, sheriff."

"Tom, I'm sure Cleatus told you about the shooting."

"Yes, Billy, he did. But as Justice of the Peace, the killing was out of my jurisdiction. If he died on the highway, then you need to call the constable or the highway patrol."

"Yes, Tom, but Robert Earl lives in Spur, your town. That makes it your territory."

"Sheriff, do you remember Isaiah Smith?"

"Yes, why do you ask?"

"About ten years ago Robert Earl and his wife were at a house dance east of town. Isaiah Smith started making advances to Mrs. Turner, or, at least, Robert Earl thought he was. When Robert Earl got through with him, Isaiah was sliced up like cantaloupe at a picnic, or bacon hanging at the meat market. It didn't kill him, but as soon as he was able, Isaiah joined the church and found Jesus. When he was baptized, the water was bloody, but Isaiah didn't care.

He really didn't want to die before he got saved. To this day he avoids drinking and dancing, and Robert Earl."

With a quaver in his voice, Tom continued, "Billy, do you know how many men Robert Earl has killed?"

"No, I don't. Every time I hear the story, it seems to double in number."

"Well, he was a Marine in the great war, and used to brag about how many Japs he'd killed in the Pacific."

"What has that got to do with anything?" questioned Billy.

"Well, if he's only killed half as many as he says, I'd call him a ruthless killer who isn't afraid to kill again."

"Tom, I'm not going to continue this discussion. Can I count on you to assist me?"

"Let's give it a day or two. I don't believe anybody else has been with his wife. If they have, we'll find out in a few days."

"I'll sleep on it. The highway patrol should be back in Dickens tomorrow. That should be soon enough," said the sheriff.

Arriving at home, Billy was greeted by Thelma. It was clear that she'd been talking to Dorothy.

"William Leroy, what are you going to do about Robert Earl?"

"What do you mean?" asked Billy.

"Just because you got a trophy today is no reason to go off and get yourself killed trying to arrest Robert Earl. Don't be a hero. I'm sorry about Joe Bob, but I don't want you to join him in the cemetery. Besides, do you know how many men Robert Earl has killed?"

"Thelma, it doesn't matter. I have a job to do and sooner or later I'm going to have to do that job. *Dorothy seems to be as scared as Cleatus.* I think I can take care of myself, with a little help. I'm going to organize a group tomorrow."

The next morning, Billy walked into the jailhouse and started talking to Cleatus.

"Have you ever been turkey hunting?"

"Billy, you know that I have. Why do you ask?"

"As smart as a turkey is, how do you get it? You have to set a trap, right?"

"What are you getting at, sheriff?"

"If Robert Earl shot Joe Bob because he was fooling around with his wife, what if we told everyone you was also involved with her?"

Cleatus turned the color of a blanched chicken, a bit green around the face. Stammering he said, "I don't think that is a good idea. Dorothy wouldn't like it either."

"Then what do you suggest?"

"Why not surprise him, like the officers who caught Bonnie and Clyde?"

"What do you mean, Cleatus?"

"Well, sheriff, have someone he recognizes buy a bottle of whiskey. When Robert Earl makes the delivery, you could catch him then."

After much pleading, Cleatus convinced Billy that he didn't want to be a paramour to Robert Earl's wife, even in name only.

"Who can we get to order the bourbon?" asked Billy. "It's got to be someone that Robert Earl knows, or he'll suspect trouble."

"My cousin John Albert usually places an order every Christmas and Fourth of July. I could get him to make the call," said Cleatus. The trap was set for sundown.

After the call was made, John agreed to leave the five-dollar bill in the lone mailbox about one-quarter mile west of town. Robert Earl would drop off the bourbon and pick up the money thirty minutes later.

"We're going to have to walk and hide before he arrives, because if we drove, he'd see the cars parked," said the sheriff.

Billy, Cleatus, Tom and the highway patrolman agreed to walk and hide in the hedge just beyond the rise in the bar ditch, a few feet from the mailbox.

As if on cue, Robert Earl arrived to the shouts of the officers. He was so surprised that he offered no resistance. With all his bootleg money, Robert Earl hired a big, Lubbock lawyer who pled self-defense for him.

Robert Earl maintained that he was protecting his wife from a philanderer. Because Robert Earl was defending his wife, he got a year in the penitentiary and three years' probation.

Cleatus, who had a case of nerves for a week or so, drank the confiscated bourbon. Billy won reelection handily.

THE SANTA CLAUSE ROBBERY

Richard Green stepped into the lobby of the First National Bank of Crosbyton just before closing at four o'clock. Dressed in his clean, pressed overalls, Richard walked with marked determination. Thirty-five years old, clean-shaven, six feet tall with blue eyes and brown hair, he knew what he wanted to do.

Fifteen years had passed since the opening of the bank in 1910, but little had changed. The small lobby had a teller's booth, straight chairs for the customers, a mahogany railing separating the secretary's desk from the main area, and a small office further back behind her desk. Back of the teller's window at the far end of the building, a vault was visible.

Lucy Taylor, the bank secretary spoke, "Good afternoon, Richard. What may I do for you?"

"I'd like to see Mr. Jones about renewing my bank note."

"We are just about to close, but I'm sure he'll make time for you. Have a seat and I'll tell him you are waiting."

Sitting down, Richard nodded to the lone teller, Simon Smith. "How are you, Simon?"

"Fine. I enjoyed your wife's Sunday school lesson yesterday. I don't know how she has the time to take care of the kids, keep the house, and teach a class, too."

"She likes to stay busy, and whatever she wants to do is fine with me. I want her to be happy."

Lucy knocked on the door of the shuttered office. Wallace Jones, an older man with gray temples, a small paunch, and kindly eyes, looked up from his desk.

"Richard Taylor is here to see you, Mr. Jones."

"Well, send him in. I need a break from the paperwork."

Rising from his chair, Mr. Jones extended his hand to the young man. "How are you, Richard? How's the family?"

Before Richard could answer, or close the door to the office, a band of three men dressed in Santa Clause suits rushed into the building. From his vantage point, Richard could survey the activity. Armed with pistols, each man had a specific job, and executed it like a seasoned professional. One Santa locked the bank doors and turned the "Closed" sign in the window. After closing the blinds, he remained by the door, a lookout Richard supposed. The other two Santas approached the teller cage. One threw a canvas bag on the counter and demanded all the money, while the third Santa walked toward the vault.

Richard turned to look at Simon, the thin, middle-aged clerk, who stood frozen at his window, unable to respond to the Santa's demand. "Did you hear me?" asked the Santa. With that, the Santa cocked his pistol and aimed it at Simon. "Now, fill the bag."

"What's going on?" Mr. Jones demanded. Circling around Richard he came out of his office. The third Santa spoke to the banker. "Get over here and fill this bag with the money from your vault. You there," motioning his pistol at Richard and Lucy, "you, too, get on the floor and lie face down, if you don't want to get hurt."

Mr. Jones walked to the vault and filled the bag. Handing it to the Santa, Mr. Jones, more out of habit than anything else, pushed the vault door shut. As the bag swept by the Santa's face, the mask was knocked askew. Voicing an alarm at being exposed, the Santa yelled at Mr. Jones.

"You stupid fool. Do you see what you've done? Don't look at me if you expect to live." Mr. Jones avoided eye contact, but the commotion caused Richard to glance up briefly. He recognized Joe Bob Thornton, a stranger he'd met at cattle auctions. Lucy, apparently still terrified, remained face down.

Through the corner of his eye, Richard saw Joe Bob angrily adjust his mask and start for the front door. Before stepping out the door, Joe Bob spoke, "No one had better open this door or alert the sheriff for five full minutes." As Richard listened, Joe Bob continued, "If any of you choose to tell the sheriff who you think I am, I will see that you and your family are killed before there is a trial." The last Santa out the door slammed it shut.

After the five minute period, Simon ran to the sheriff's office. His deputy was in the office and ran back with Simon to confirm what had happened and alert the sheriffs in the neighboring towns, requesting roadblocks. No one was sure which direction the robbers had gone.

After answering the initial questions of the deputy, Richard spoke, "I recognized the third robber. His name is Joe Bob Thornton. I've seen him at farm auctions in Rotan."

Realizing the gravity of Richard's statement, Mr. Jones, spoke, "Richard, you have the most to lose. The gunmen know that I will talk because I own the bank, but I can't tell the officials much. The sheriff will be watching out for the bank, but you could be in great danger. Knowing that you will be called to testify in court could bring harm to you and your family. Get out of town until these rascals are caught."

The local sheriff notified the Texas Rangers and the sheriffs in the neighboring counties. The robbers' descriptions, though vague, was broadcast. Roadblocks at Dickens, Aspermont, and Idalou were manned by the various law enforcement bodies looking for three men in red suits, although, logically the men would discard the suits immediately after leaving the bank. The get-away car, a 1920 Ford Model A, could not travel very far nor very fast without being seen.

Realizing the full impact of what Mr. Jones had said, Richard mounted his horse and rode as quickly as he could to his farm. When he arrived, the sun was setting on this December afternoon.

"Julie, the bank was robbed while I was talking to Mr. Jones."

"Was anybody hurt?" asked his wife looking at Richard for any signs of injury.

Taking a deep breath, Richard paused before continuing, "I want you to be quiet and listen to me. No one was hurt, but I can identify one of the men. It was Joe Bob Thornton, from the White River community. He said he'd kill me, and all my family, if I identified him in a court of law."

"Oh, my," said Julie, sitting down in a nearby chair. "What are we going to do?"

"I want you to take the kids and get out of here as soon as possible."

"But, what about you? My place is with you."

"No, your place is with the kids. They need you now."

Looking deeply into her eyes, Richard said, "I can get by. I plan to go into hiding as soon as I know that you and the kids are okay. Now, I want you to get your things together as quickly as possible, catch the nine o'clock train to Lubbock, and then, buy a ticket for Amarillo. It is unlikely that the gunmen will be looking for you, since they would be looking for a couple with kids. Besides, they don't know your folks' name. If someone is watching, buy the ticket for Amarillo. Then get off the train at Tulia. It's better if you don't know where I am. I will contact you when things are safe. Hurry, now, please."

"What are you going to do?"

"I'll ride out on Toby. There are plenty of big ranches that will hire a stray cowboy. When things calm down, or the men are caught, I'll write you. Hurry."

Julie packed mainly for the three kids. Throwing a few things for herself, she drove the wagon to town, leaving it at a friend's house. Boarding the train, she was apprehensive that she was watched. Richard remained in the shadows, waiting to be sure the family was safely on the train. He was ready to assist Julie if the need arose. His gun was loaded.

The darkness aided Richard and Julie's departure. Richard was satisfied they were safe on the train as it slowly pulled away from the station. He then turned his horse eastward and faded into the darkness.

The big ranches in the area have a geographical escarpment, which divides the high plains from the south plains. The cliffs and gullies of the Cap Rock provide excellent grazing for cattle, as well as a home for rattlesnakes and bank robbers. People could hide in the rolling land of mesquite trees and red, clay hills for years, provided they were not snake bit.

After camping out for two days and traveling steadily, Richard rode through the gates of the Pitchfork Ranch, about twenty miles west of Guthrie. He could see the lights of the bunkhouse for several miles. He rode Toby up to the cook shack and dismounted, hoping to find employment and an evening meal. Supper had been over for some time, but the cowboys liked to linger over their coffee on these long, winter nights.

Several cowboys heard his approach and stepped outside to greet him. "Howdy, stranger, what brings you to this neck of the woods?"

"Howdy, I'm looking for work. Do you need any extra hands now?" asked Richard as he dismounted.

Mr. Rawlins, the foreman, stepped forward out of the door's light and said, "As a matter of fact, we do need some help. We are repairing the fences before the spring roundup.

The spread is so large, we can't do the job without some extra help. Where are you from?"

"I recently left Matador when the ranch owner died," Richard lied.

"Oh, have you been cowboying long?"

"Yes, sir, about fifteen years."

"What is your name?"

"Tom Clayton."

"All right, Tom, I'll try you out beginning tomorrow morning. If you work out, you've got a job as long as you want it." Mr. Rawlins stepped over and shook Richard's hand.

"Thanks."

A young, lanky cowboy, standing in the group listening to the conversation, was calmly rolling his own smokes. Mr. Rawlins looked at him and said, "Billy Wayne, show Tom where to keep his horse. Afterwards, if he wants some cold beans or hot coffee, bring him back here, and then take him over to the bunkhouse."

"Yes, sir."

"See you in the morning," said Mr. Rawlins, turning and walking away.

"Thanks," said Richard, talking to the man's shadow.

Every month, when payday rolled around, the cowboys went to town. Richard, who proved to be a better cowboy than his boss anticipated, continued to work on the ranch. When he went to town with the other men, he inquired discreetly about Joe Bob.

"Yes," said the sheriff, "we are still looking for Joe Bob. The robbers traveled to Aspermont before meeting a roadblock; gunfire was exchanged, and two of the men were killed. In the darkness, Job Bob Thornton melted into the pastureland, taking the bank's money with him. As bad as the brush is in that area, it would take men, horses, and dogs days, weeks, or even months to find him." By Richard's reckoning, it had almost been four months.

※

During the spring roundup, when the cowboys found the mother cows and brought their calves to be branded, Billy Wayne Compton, who was in the far reaches of the south pasture, noticed a fire burning in a distant ravine. Expecting cattle rustlers who could be branding the ranch herd, he rode up on the man who was roasting a pig over the open fire.

"Howdy," said Billy Wayne. "Mister, what are you doing on this ranch? Are you lost?"

Dirty and needing a shave, haircut and clean clothes, Joe Bob glanced at the mounted cowboy. "Yes, sir, I reckon I'm lost. I killed this feral hog and this is the first decent meal I've had in a long time. I haven't killed or bothered your cattle. During the last cold spell my horse spooked and ran away. I was hoping to find a ranch house around here. Would you care to join me for lunch?"

"No, thanks. As a lark, a few of us cowboys killed and roasted a wild pig some time ago. The meat was tough and tasted horrible. I don't think I want any more of it. I found some hard tack in my saddlebags and ate it a while ago.

When you finish, I think we need to get to headquarters and help you get your bearings."

After the hungry stranger finished his meal of hog meat, Joe Bob agreed to follow Billy back to the ranch house, on the stringer Billy had. He always took a spare horse so he could swap when the one he was riding was spent.

———— ⬥ ————

That night, the first thing that Richard did when he got to the ranch house was rub Toby down. While he was working on Toby, he glanced up to see Billy and a stranger

LNEAGLE

riding in. As the two got nearer, Richard recognized the second rider. He reached over the horse's mane and pulled the rifle from its holster. All the cowboys had rifles for killing snakes and varmints on the spread. *It looks like I've found a use for the rifle after all.*

As Joe Bob dismounted, Richard took aim, cocked the 3030's hammer, and said, "Hands up." Joe Bob offered little resistance.

Stiffening and lifting his hands, he turned toward Richard. "I might have known it was you." Watching the encounter from the porch, Mr. Rawlins stepped over to the men.

Richard, guessing the question on his face said, "Mr. Rawlins, this man is Joe Bob Thornton. He robbed the bank at Crosbyton and has been on the run ever since. Someone needs to notify Sheriff Moore in Crosbyton."

Mr. Rawlins, satisfied with the explanation, phoned Crosbyton. The sheriff and two deputies came as soon as they could and took custody of Joe Bob. "Where's the money?"

"It's in the saddle bags. There isn't much to spend it on out here in the wilds."

Looking around at the other men who had gathered, Sheriff Moore recognized Richard. He nodded at him. Turning to Mr. Rawlins the sheriff said, "There's a reward for Joe Bob's capture. Who gets the check?"

"Tom Clayton, here," said Mr. Rawlins.

Sheriff Moore said, "That's not Tom Clayton, that's Richard Green."

Richard turned to face Mr. Rawlins. "I'm sorry I had to lie to you, but Joe Bob said he'd kill me and all my family. It's harder to find a man, if he changes his name." Turning back to the sheriff, Richard asked, "How much is the reward?"

"$10,000."

Richard smiled, That was enough to pay off the note and farm another year.

Mr. Rawlins spoke, "Give the money to Mr. Green, Sheriff. He's a good hand whatever handle he goes by." Turning to Richard he added, "You're a good man, Tom, or Richard. If you ever need work, you've got a job here."

Richard replied, "Thanks, Mr. Rawlins, I'll keep that in mind." I think I'll split the money with Billy, too. After all, he brought the crook to me.

On Saturday, Richard got his check, quit his job and wired Julie to bring the kids home.

THE PRECINCT ELECTION

While finishing his breakfast, Brother Calvin Joshua Hill reviewed his first sermon to be delivered that day to his flock at Dickens City. The phone rang. Opal Jean returned to the kitchen from the hall, "A man wants to talk to you."

"Did you get his name?"

"Yes, Cal, but I don't think you know him. He said he was Shorty Sharp."

"Opal Jean, you know I don't like to be interrupted while I am studying my notes. Why didn't you tell him I'd call him after church?"

"He seemed pretty determined to talk to you. He's waiting."

Laying his sermon on the breakfast table, Cal got up and walked to the hall phone. "Hello, this is Brother Hill. How can I help you?"

"Brother Hill? This is Shorty Sharp. I need to talk to you, but I want it to be secret, if possible. Would you meet me out west of town after dark, say nine o'clock?"

"Yes, I guess I can. The evening service will be over by then. Where do you want to meet?"

"There's an old house about two miles west of town. I'll keep my car lights on so you can find me."

"Fine. I'll plan on being there by nine."

"Thanks, Reverend," said Shorty, hanging up the phone.

Puzzled, Opal Jean studied her husband. "What did he want?"

"He wants to see me tonight after church. Now, keep this to yourself. I think I may add another soul to my flock." Cal returned to his notes and finished off his coffee.

Calvin Joshua Hill, tall and thin, having brown hair and eyes, had spent the majority of his life going to school and preparing for the ministry. The pastoral search committee, upon the recommendation of his mentor at Hardin-Simmons University, had recommended Cal for this first appointment. Being young and recently married, Calvin fit the requirements for the pastorate at Dickens City: young, poor, and manageable by the deacons of the First Baptist Church.

Calvin knew when he married Opal Jean, also a Hardin-Simmons graduate, that his life would be changed forever. If Opal had her way, he'd become another Billy Graham. In the short month since they'd married, he'd heard her say that with her help and drive they were going to be successful. His cooperation was requested.

Together they comprised a team, well, a team, he guessed, of innocents to serve their first call. Glancing at Opal Jean, he smiled. She was still young enough to believe that life was beautiful. Her personal credo was that all people, if given the chance, would be honest in their relationships, especially churchwomen. And, if they disappointed her, then she'd make a list, turn it over to him, and he, in turn would submit the list to God.

Grabbing the pages of his carefully typed sermon, Calvin prepared to face the field ripe unto harvest. "Opal, please help me with this tie. It doesn't seem to want to behave."

"We'll go together, if you'll give me five minutes. I want us to make a good impression on these folks. Remember, dear, today is the first day of your brilliant career."

Sighing, Cal replied, "Yes, dear."

Arriving early for the Sunday school assembly, Bro. Cal and Opal felt the eyes of the crowd upon them at the gathering. Everybody knew who they were; for some reason, " the lambs prepared for slaughter" floated through his mind. But not today. Today, a sort of peace prevailed similar to the dawn before a major battle.

After the hymns were sung, the collection taken, and the number of Bibles counted, Elder Obid stood up to speak. Dramatically emptying a sack of glass beer bottles on to the hardwood floor at the front of the church, Obid began. "Brothers and sisters, the Legislature of the State of Texas has just passed a law granting each precinct the right to determine whether it can sell hard liquor, or remain dry and dedicated to God's word. We don't want our roads and bar ditches cluttered with whiskey bottles and beer cans, do we?"

"No," roared the church members unanimously.

"I've heard it on good authority that Dickens City is one of the first precincts to have a vote. It takes three months to gather the number of signatures and then three months to have the vote. This is a struggle between good and evil. If we allow this sin to infiltrate this God-fearing community, then Heaven help Dickens City."

After the roar of 'Amen's' had settled, Nathan Pritchett, not one to be easily led, asked, "Brother Obid, where did you find all those bottles and cans?"

"My boys and I picked them up on the way to church this morning."

"Well, if they were already here, what is the commotion all about?"

Bro. Obid cut his eyes at Nathan, "If it is this bad now, just imagine how much worse is can be once the criminal elements and the big city liquor stores move into our fair city." Nathan joined the quiet congregation.

After the assembly, Cal breathed a sigh of relief as the members filed out of the sanctuary to their classes. The members, upon hearing the piano start playing, knew to return for the worship service. Cal could tell by their faces that every word the teachers had spoken was anti-climatic. After the service started, it seemed the songs were, too. During the pastoral prayer, Cal pleaded with God to save their fair community, their state and their country; he knew full well that no one heard a word of the prayer.

At the conclusion of the service, everyone in the congregation bragged about the sermon, Cal wondered if it was to give the preacher enough rope to hang himself, or improve. He had heard a similar axiom from his dad: If the chief contributor to the church has a wife who cannot safely carry a tune, the polite thing to do is brag on her singing, praying that it will improve.

Brother Cal observed the car lights as he drove up to the abandoned house. He noticed a short, stocky man in his late fifties getting out of his new Oldsmobile. When Calvin drove up, he rolled the window down and came to a stop.

"Reverend Hill," said the cigar-smoking man, "I'm Shorty Sharp. I am happy we could get together."

"Well, Mr. Sharp, " replied Cal, "First of all, are you a member of my church?"

"My mother is a member, but I'm not. Her arthritis keeps her at home more than she likes."

"I wasn't sure if I had met her at the services."

"No, she wasn't there, but I'm sure you'll meet her soon."

"Mr. Sharp, what can I do for you, and why are we meeting here like this?"

"Reverend, I have an unsavory reputation in Dickens City. This is why I asked to meet with you at night."

"Mr. Sharp, all are equal in the eyes of God. What do you want?"

Mr. Sharp stepped closer to Cal and spoke, "As you probably know, Dickens City is ripe for a precinct vote."

"Yes, that's what I've heard. What I don't understand is why."

"It's about one hundred and twenty-five miles to the nearest wet town."

"What town is that?"

"Wichita Falls, or as we say Whiskey-taw Falls. If the precinct votes wet, it will put the bootleggers out of business. We'll have liquor stores selling beer and wine and all kinds of spirits. Do you want that to happen here in Dickens City?"

"Of course not." said Bro. Cal.

"I didn't think you would. The last thing we need is to make the selling of liquor a legitimate business. I called several of my associates last week when we saw the story in the Lubbock *Avalanche Journal.* They asked me to be the spokesman for the group."

"What kind of group are we talking about?"

"Preacher, don't you know who I am?"

"No, I just assumed you were a concerned citizen."

"Let's just leave it at that."

After a moment, Calvin interjected, "But Dickens City is a small town, less than four hundred people live here."

"It has a large trade area and it would provide liquor for a number of people who are within driving distance. Our group of concerned citizens have pledged to give you and the First Baptist Church one hundred thousand dollars to help you with your campaign. Here is the initial deposit of twenty thousand. Whenever you need money for posters, sign boards, bill boards or radio spots, however you choose to spend the money, we all stand behind you one hundred percent."

"Why, Brother Sharp, that is a noteworthy thing to do," said the Reverend. "What I don't see is why you won't let me tell the folks about your generosity."

"Reverend, you're new to the town. When you find out what I do for a living, I'm sure you will understand. Here's the cash. Please spend it to get the best bang for the buck."

"God bless you, Brother Sharp," replied Calvin as he pocketed the cash. "Can we expect to see you in the services next Sunday?"

"No, pastor. Thanks anyway, but Sunday is my day of rest."

"I'd like to tell folks about your good deed."

"That information might offend some of the members. I'd rather you not reveal the source, unless it is absolutely necessary."

"Thanks again for your act of kindness."

Abruptly leaving, Shorty sped away into the night.

***

Opal Jean met Cal at the door when he returned. "Calvin, do you know what Mr. Sharp does for a living? I'll tell you. He's a bootlegger, that's what. What did he want with you?"

Well, that explains Bro. Sharp's cryptic comments. Cal thought. Aloud, he said, "Now, now, Opal dear, you know I can't tell you that. I will say that he made a big decision to help the community, and his mother is a member of our church."

"What do you mean by a big decision? Did you point out the errors of his ways?"

Calvin, fingering the money in his pocket, smiled and said, "Now, Opal, the Lord works in mysterious ways. He gave me a contribution, but you can't talk to anyone about it."

"Calvin, you can't accept that money. It is ill-gotten gains. The Lord doesn't want tainted money. You need to return it."

Pleading, Cal said, "Didn't Jesus say it was more blessed to give than receive? All we are doing is helping Mr. Sharp be blessed."

"Calvin, I thought you were a superior man, but if you take that money, you are sorry as you can be."

"Now, now, Opal dear, don't you remember in Bible 101, that if a prostitute tithed her tenth to the church, that she was okay in the eyes of God?"

"Hog wash. We haven't finished the discussion about this," said Opal as she slammed the bathroom door in Calvin's face.

The next morning, Calvin met with the church secretary to add his money to the church collection. Sister Caruthers spoke, "I'm puzzled. Why would a stranger offer to help us do God's Work?"

"Maybe it's out of the goodness of his heart. Have you contacted any of the other churches to help with the campaign?"

The bank teller, Sister Thelma said, "There used to be a ministerial alliance here in the community. The churches tried to have one several years ago, but there are so few churches and so few members that the plan was scrapped."

"Maybe we should resurrect it, provided there is an election. We are going to need all the help we can get if we want to win."

"I can give you a list of the preachers in the area. Naturally, they will all be against the vote, except those Lutherans. Since our church is the largest, you should spearhead the anti-drink campaign."

With the money gathered, all that was left for Calvin to do was marshal the city's youth. After the Baptist Young People's Union made the posters, the Epworth League agreed to carry them door-to-door, while the Presbyterian group would make phone calls to the citizenry.

Meanwhile, the opposition representing the liquor lobby hired a big, high-powered lawyer—Caleb Brumett. His big, black Buick attracted attention even before he stepped out of the car.

John Carpenter, a faithful member of Cal's church, reported to Calvin about the comings and goings of the enemy. John noted that the first thing Brumett did was call on the abstract office in the Dickens County Courthouse, looking for the names and addresses of the owners of every vacant lot, or abandoned house, in the city. Usually, the county clerk, Thelma Watson, or the county judge, George House, are friendly and cordial to visitors. Perceived as the opposition, this particular lawyer was too slick and, obviously, up to no good. Besides, he didn't spend the night, but hurried back home to Wichita Falls. As he pulled out of the parking lot at the courthouse, Thelma called Calvin and reported.

Two weeks later, the purpose of the visit was revealed. Roy Bob's cousin, Luther Joe, a trailer house salesman in Lubbock, called. Walking rapidly, Roy Bob reached the church completely out of breath.

"Brother Cal, Brother Cal," heaved Roy Bob.

"What is it, Brother Roy?"

"My cousin is making money faster than he can write up the orders for used trailers."

"What are you talking about?"

"A group of investors from Wichita went to Lubbock a week ago and are buying every trailer they can get their hands on."

"Roy Bob, I'm happy for your cousin, but why are you telling me this?"

"Preacher, they are planning on moving those trailers to Dickens City. If a person lives in a trailer house for six months, they are eligible to vote in the election. I've also heard that the big money interests and liquor dealers are looking for widows in Guthrie, Matador, and Spur to pay them to live in their houses so they can win the election."

"Well, I don't think very many widows would vote wet."

"When you add a small salary to their social security checks to live in our fair city, yes, I believe we are in trouble."

As moderator, Cal called the brotherhood together, "Men, we've got to count heads to be sure we can win this vote. Leroy, you and Grady Joe count the trailers as they move into Dickens. Jimmy, you and Billy tally the votes we have right now. I doubt that we can change the minds of many voters, but we can pray for them."

Overnight, billboards sprang up. "For the sake of my family, I'll vote dry." was countered with, "Take a little wine for thy stomach's sake." Still other placards stated, "Be not deceived, God is not mocked." To be countered with, "Wine maketh glad the heart."

Posters were seen on the lawns of the true believers, mainly the Baptists. The county clerk's office was busy with the tax rolls and the new landowners in town. The grocery store expanded its hours and its services. The two gas stations were setting new sales records daily. It was a boomtown, at least for a while.

Several times Cal phoned Shorty for more money. No questions were asked about how it would be used; it was simply delivered in brown bags at night and left on the parsonage's porch.

Drawn and haggard, Calvin looked like he'd lost his last battle with a herd of raging buffalo. Elder Obid said, "Brother Calvin, I thought you were up to this campaign, but it looks like you are worn out."

"I am. I don't seem to have enough energy to go around. The election is next week, and I'm not sure we have the votes to defeat it. Surely God in His wisdom will hear us and come to our aid."

"We can only do so much, the rest is in God's hands."

"Could we win, if all the Christians voted dry?"

"Yes, but you know those Lutherans. They will openly support us, but will vote against us in the election, just like Granny Grimes. She claims that liquor is medicinal, but everyone knows she likes to drink. Demon rum is at the bottom of their hearts. The only people we can count on are the bootleggers."

"Well, God bless the bootleggers, they are serving a good purpose, at least for now."

The Election Day finally came to a close. Opal Jean woke her husband to come to the supper table. He'd been asleep in his favorite chair.

Looking up at her, Cal heard the phone ring. Reaching over to the table, he answered. "Preacher," said the voice on the line. "This is Shorty. We lost by one vote. The election judge recounted the votes three times. The wets won."

"Thank you for letting me know. I do appreciate your help."

Looking up at Opal Jean, Calvin said, "Well, we lost this election."

"Maybe we shouldn't have taken Mr. Sharp's money. It was tainted, you know, " she said sweetly.

"Now, look here," said the Reverend. "I prayed over that money and asked God to bless us with it. Besides, Christ allowed Mary Magdalene to wash his feet, even though many thought she had a questionable reputation. Once that money reaches the church, it's okay."

"Yes, dear," she said, "but Billy Graham wouldn't have taken the money."

"Dr. Graham wasn't fighting for the decency of Dickens City, either."

"Well," said Opal, "if you are going to be a world renowned preacher, you better watch out for bootlegger's money next time."

Sighing as if to exhale the world's problems in one breath, Calvin muttered, "Yes, dear."

THE ANNUAL RABBIT HUNT

Billy Joe Stovall, the pharmacist, leaned against the counter facing Leo Jones and Clifford Moore. Billy was an intense man, thin, of average height, who dreaded this time of year because he was nearly killed in the last two rabbit hunts. Facing both Leo and Clifford, he gave the impression of a child in a dentist's chair: fear.

Leo Jones and Clifford Moore were sitting in the drug store drinking coffee, as they had done each morning for the past twenty years. The farmers were killing time waiting for the ground to dry out so their crops would sprout and grow. Leo, heavy set with thinning gray hair and a paunch, gave the appearance of a successful middle-aged man. Clifford, younger and more robust, was of average height, with blue eyes and dark brown hair.

"It's about time that we set the date for the rabbit hunt. I've seen some of them coming into the fields looking for food already," said Leo.

"Yes, this rain we had will bring them out," agreed Cliff.

The Croton Brakes, a natural geological escarpment, was a clear demarcation of the land, dividing the ranch

land from the tillable soil. When the rains came, there was an abundance of rats and snakes. The snakes make quick work of the rats. The rabbits, having few predators, would come out of the ranching area down in the canyons and feed on the newly-planted crops. In order for the farmers to save their crops, a rabbit hunt was organized annually. The farmers killed what the foxes and wolves did not devour.

Turning pale, Billy Joe said, "A-a-aren't we rruh-shing the date a bit? Why not w-wuh-wait until a little later in the year?" Billy Joe's speech betrayed the fear in his entire body, improving immediately after the yearly hunt.

"Oh, Billy, it takes you three weeks after each hunt to calm down enough so that you can talk without stuttering. Don't be such a sissy," said Cliff.

"I'm not a sissy. Those two incidents in the last two years could have killed me…or somebody else."

Leo replied, "Look, it was an innocent mistake. Old man Hindman forgot to watch where he was stepping when we formed our line and walked the fields to scare up the rabbits. Just because he forgot where the old cistern was and stepped into it is little cause to complain. He accidentally shot his rifle when he fell. That's no reason to give up on the hunt. Besides, all he got from the accident were a few bruises. That old cistern has been dry for twenty-five years."

Billy Joe solemnly spoke, "Well, I'm glad he didn't hurt himself when he fell in, but he ruined my felt hat. There are bullet holes all over the crown and brim. If he'd shot a little lower, I wouldn't be here today. I'm convinced hunting is too dangerous for a group of men who aren't paying attention."

"Well, we started out too early in the morning. He said he couldn't see the cistern because it was too dark," replied Cliff.

"It was too dark, but if you want to catch the rabbits, you need to be there early when they are feeding on our crops," added Leo.

Looking directly at Billy Joe, Cliff continued, "The second time you got shot at could have happened to anyone. Mr. Moore got tired of walking and sat down to get the sand out of his shoes and rest a spell. When Odis scared up a rabbit and it took off, who was to know that it was headed straight for John's overalls and ran up his pant leg? He got rattled and shot just to scare the rabbit."

"It didn't work properly. It scared me and I'll carry to my grave the scars the doctor made taking the buckshot out of my shoulder."

"Well, I'm sure he didn't mean to hurt anyone."

Rubbing his scarred shoulder, Billy Joe answered, "I agree, and I'm not sure what I'd do if something ran up my britches."

"Mr. Moore said he thought it was a snake. Of course, in the early dawn, it could have been anything."

"Naturally, I've forgiven both of them, that's the least I could do, but firing a shotgun without thinking is irresponsible," said Billy Joe.

"The problem," interrupted Leo, "is that our community is so small. We need every able-bodied man to help us save our crops from the varmints, that includes people who aren't as careful as they should be."

"Remember the year when Clyde Harris had been drinking all night and showed up the morning of the hunt? In between fighting sleep and shooting at shadows that moved, Clyde scared a number of us," recalled Leo. "But I don't know the answer to that problem. I guess we could give the drunks and old people blank shells."

Clifford intoned, "Maybe we ought to exempt some people. Some of the old-timers maybe should sit it out."

"How do you draw the line on old people?" questioned Leo. "Old man Russell can shoot a squirrel a half-mile away. I want him to help us kill the rabbits."

"Well, we can't arbitrarily make a rule unless we all vote on it. Anyway, someone is bound to get his feelings hurt, either way we vote."

"Yes," nodded Billy Joe, "but we might save lives."

When Billy Joe noticed a lull in the conversation, Leo introduced another problem. "What about the wear-and-tear on our dogs? Inez gave me a registered retriever for my birthday. During last year's hunt, Molly was working like she was supposed to, pointing at some bushes. She happened to turn around just as Homer was aiming his gun. The site on the barrel was out of adjustment, and Homer aimed low. He filled Molly's rear end with buckshot. Now, every time I take her out to hunt, she is afraid I will shoot her and she won't point like she's supposed to. I'm going to have to give her away. I don't blame Homer, but it was a dumb thing to do. It sure ruined a good bird dog."

"Maybe I should be exempt, too, except I want to be one of the regular guys," said Billy Joe. "My wife doesn't care if I don't hunt, but I do. I just don't want to get hurt."

"And we really want you to hunt with us, Billy Joe," laughed Cleo, "you just can't tell what will happen to you. Seems like you're a time bomb waiting to go off."

"There ought to be a better way, or someone will be killed, and I don't want to be the one to prove the point," pleaded Billy Joe.

"Well, it is a good time for fellowship. Our wives cook a great meal, we get rid of the varmints, we get to work our dogs, and we've got a chance to visit with our neighbors."

"I still wish there was a safer way to solve the problem," sighed Billy Joe.

Elmer Dee Watson, the local hardware dealer, was concerned with sales.

How can I sell more guns, if everyone already has a gun?

Mrs. Lilly, Elmer's wife, had heard the topic discussed several times. While she did not have an answer, she had an idea.

"Elmer, the grownups have guns, what about the kids? How could we get the parents to buy them guns?"

"Suppose we had a bounty on the rabbits?" said Elmer Dee.

"Would that interfere with the game warden?"

"I don't see why it should. I'll talk to him before we do anything, but you may have a great idea for increasing sales."

Paul Dale Smith, the game warden, said he saw no problem with a private concern, such as a hardware store, offering a bounty for rabbit hides.

Without hesitation, Paul Dale put a big poster in his store window, "Rabbit pelts bought here: Five for $10 dollars. You buy the shells, I'll loan you the shotgun."

Elmer also ran an ad in the local paper. The word spread among the high school boys like a prairie fire before a rain. For the boys whose parents would not allow them to borrow Paul's gun, they had to be inventive: some used skunk traps and beaver traps, some used sticks and dogs, some used sling shots, although the dogs usually were more successful than the boys.

In a short time, many of the youth were rabbit hunting with borrowed rifles, either their fathers' guns or Elmer Dee's loaner.

<hr />

In a very short time, the surviving rabbits left the community for safer environs. To the town fathers' delight, no youth was injured except Billy Joe's boy, who accidentally broke his leg trying to jump a barbed-wire fence while holding his shotgun.

Billy Joe, for one, was relieved that he did not have to go on any more hunts in order to be one of the good old boys. His time bomb was diffused. Besides, it was more pleasant to sit around the drug store and tell tales, than it was to be looking down the rifle barrel of someone who is armed and ready to shoot.

The parents, for the most part, bought the loaned rifles for their sons, and Elmer Dee had a great season. Some boys used their first kills as a down payment on their own shotgun.

Billy Joe knew, in spite of Cliff's complaining that he'd keep his dog. Billy Joe quit stuttering after he was exempt from the rabbit hunts.

Let the youths take care of the rabbit problem; I'll run the drug store.

ABOUT THE AUTHOR

Born in rural West Texas in the middle of the last century, Michael Hairgrove has attempted to recreate a simpler time and express some of the rich experiences he had growing up in Spur, Texas.

Before retiring in 2003, Mike taught English in the

Michael Hairgrove

Texas Public Schools for twenty-five years. He includes reading, writing, and walking his beagle as primary hobbies.

While teaching at Texas A & M, he met and married the love of his life, Betty Belvin Hairgrove. When they married, Mike got the added bonus of two step-children, Patricia and Anne Elizabeth. Today, Mike lives in the same house he's lived in for the past forty years with his beagle Reginald.

Photo by Marty Mitchell

.